MARRIAGE TRIAGE

MARRIAGE TRIAGE

A GUIDE TO HEALING FOR THE HURTING SPOUSE

STEPHEN GOODE

Ambassador International
Greenville, South Carolina & Belfast, Northern Ireland
www.ambassador-international.com

Marriage Triage
A Guide to Healing for the Hurting Spouse

© 2012 by Stephen Goode
All rights reserved

Printed in the United States of America

ISBN: 978-1-62020-018-6
eISBN: 978-1-62020-051-3

Unless otherwise noted Scriptures taken from the NEW AMERICAN STANDARD BIBLE®, © Copyright 1960, 1962, 1963, 1968, 1971, 1972, 1973, 1975, 1977, 1995 by The Lockman Foundation. Used by permission. (www.Lockman.org)

Cover Design and Page Layout by Matthew Mulder

AMBASSADOR INTERNATIONAL
Emerald House
427 Wade Hampton Blvd.
Greenville, SC 29609, USA
www.ambassador-international.com

AMBASSADOR BOOKS
The Mount
2 Woodstock Link
Belfast, BT6 8DD, Northern Ireland, UK
www.ambassador-international.com

The colophon is a trademark of Ambassador

Details in some anecdotes and stories have been changed to protect the identities of the persons involved. All rights reserved. No part of this publication may be reproduced, stored in a retrieval system or transmitted in any form or by any means—electronic, mechanical, photocopy, recording, or any other—except for brief quotations in printed reviews, without the prior permission of Ambassador International. Requests for permission may be sent to publisher@emeraldhouse.com.

In Memory Of

In memory of Dr. Robert and Marie Goode, who never gave up on me. Though during my early years I manifested the traits of a stereotypical preacher's kid, they showed me unconditional love through their prayers and encouragement. They committed to raise me in the nurture and admonition of the Lord, regardless of the cost. I am eternally grateful to them and look forward to my reunion with them in heaven one day. I also dedicate this book to my sister Roxanne Goode, who died in 1964.

CONTENTS

ACKNOWLEDGMENTS 9
FOREWORD 11

CHAPTER ONE
WHAT IS MARRIAGE TRIAGE? 17

CHAPTER TWO
THE CRISIS BEGINS 31

CHAPTER THREE
GOD'S GRACE NEVER LEAVES 45

CHAPTER FOUR
OWN YOUR SINS AND FAILURES 59

CHAPTER FIVE
DOCUMENT YOUR THOUGHTS AND EXPERIENCES 75

CHAPTER SIX
COUNSEL WITH GODLY PEOPLE 85

CHAPTER SEVEN
ADAPT TO YOUR CIRCUMSTANCES 97

CHAPTER EIGHT
RESPOND BIBLICALLY 111

CHAPTER NINE
ENDURE THROUGH YOUR CIRCUMSTANCES 131

CHAPTER TEN
SHIELD YOUR HEART 155

CHAPTER ELEVEN
THE REAL PURPOSE 173

APPENDIX 185
NOTES 197
RESOURCES 199
ABOUT THE AUTHOR 201

ACKNOWLEDGMENTS

I'D LIKE TO THANK MY wife, April, who has endured through many lonely nights taking care of our children, Savannah and Noah, while I prepared this work. She has supported me and the calling God has placed on our lives. I cherish her and thank God each day for blessing me with such an awesome family. God has truly given me what I do not deserve.

To my church family at Northside Baptist, I love and thank you for welcoming me into your fellowship. For all the readers who eagerly read the manuscript and provided me content and editing feedback, I am forever in your debt.

I also owe a big thanks to my webmaster, Stephen Houchen, who in 2007 volunteered his skills and abilities to set up the TrumpetforGod.org website where *The Biblical Counseling Moment* audios are located. He helped provide the outlet for thousands to hear and be ministered to, and I am grateful for his efforts.

I thank my Lord and Savior Jesus Christ for allowing me the privilege of serving Him through this book. I can never repay the eternal gift He has freely given me. May I live out my life always striving to show my gratitude for His gift of salvation.

To all the many friends and ministry partners who have encouraged me, I thank you for being a part of this ministry. You know who you are, and if I needed a higher word count, I would name you all.

I also want to acknowledge and thank my editor, Brenda Covert, who was very patient with me as she guided me through the editing journey.

FOREWORD

WE HEAR SO MANY NEGATIVE reports documenting the state of our nation and the breakdown of the family, that when something encouraging comes along we like to ' spread the news.' Such is the case with the ministry of Christian counselor Steve Goode. Several years ago as I began to learn of Steve's ministry—serving couples and families, broadcasting, and writing—I was not only impressed but also deeply encouraged.

Steve Goode brings to the table not only biblical knowledge and professional credentials, but also years of real-world experience, having successfully helped many people through some of life's most challenging valleys.

I know Steve to be a man who serves God by serving people. Prior to becoming a Christian counselor, he served as a law-enforcement officer. On the street and now in the church, Steve Goode knows what it is like to help people through the crucible of life's experiences. And now, I believe God has positioned Rev. Goode for his most fruitful endeavor yet: Release of the Marriage Triage book.

At the time of this publication, U.S. census reports show that people are waiting longer and longer to get married. Fewer people are choosing to marry and build a traditional family. Into this void left by the retreating "two-parent, nuclear family," we see the emergence of homosexual couples, and other so-called 'alternative family' structures. The number of couples living together without benefit of marriage is increasing (which is a strong predictor of divorce later, if marriage eventually does occur). One of the greatest indicators for poverty, financial duress, at-risk behavior among youth (drugs, promiscuity, gang involvement), and a contributing factor for the high-school dropout rate, is divorce.

How serious a toll is the breakdown of the family taking on America? Think about these tragic statistics: Every day, 4,356 children below age 18 are arrested. That's 1.6 million arrests per year. As of 2012, 1 out of 8 children now in elementary school will not graduate from high school. That's 6.6 million graduate-aged youth who will not get a high-school diploma this year. Of these, 1.5 million will end up in prison. Now think about this: 98% of African American youth who do not finish high-school—will, by age 30—be in prison, or dead. Today, 1 out of 3 African American males are in prison.

What is the solution to these startling trends? What will turn these heartbreaking tides? The answer lies in one of God's greatest gifts to the human race: The family. Volumes of data prove that the hope for our children (and the hope for restoration of America) lies in stable, loving, two-parent families.

That's why Marriage Triage is such an important resource. Steve Goode has created a tool that is equipping churches and individuals to uphold God's perfect design for marriage and the family. Our nation needs strong families, and couples today need all the help they can get in navigating the murky waters of a culture that no longer affirms marriage and the home. I applaud the work of my trusted colleague, Steve Goode, and I highly recommend his research and ministry.

Alex McFarland
Director, Apologetics and Christian worldview
North Greenville University, SC
www.alexmcfarland.com

MARRIAGE TRIAGE

Triage (**tree**-ah*zh*) is the assignment of degrees of urgency to decide the order of treatment of people injured in a battle or disaster. **Marriage Triage** is a term the author has created to describe the biblical care and attention given to Christian marriages that are in a state of crisis. The crisis can be anything that has broken the biblical model of what a Christian marriage is supposed to be. The primary goal of **Marriage Triage** is to encourage the hurting spouse to make biblical choices when the temptation is to make emotional decisions.

CHAPTER ONE
WHAT IS MARRIAGE TRIAGE?

EVEN A SIMPLE FLESH WOUND needs proper care to guard against unnecessarily induced complications. Justin was only nineteen years old when he was cut by a small knife across an area between his left arm and chest. He didn't know what to do, so he began running in the direction of his home, which was a nearby apartment. Maybe Justin thought if he could just make it to the threshold of his home that everything would be okay. He had no way of knowing what he was doing to his body as he urgently put one foot in front of the other. He was on a mission to flee from the location where his injury had been inflicted. Because Justin was running, his heart was pumping as hard as it could to oxygenate his blood and organs. When he entered the door of his apartment, Justin's weakened body collapsed on the carpet from the accelerated loss of blood.

I remember driving to the apartment complex with blue lights and siren activated, unaware of the seriousness of Justin's injuries. When I arrived, the emergency personnel were doing all they could to save Justin's life. I was able to retrace where Justin first stood from a trail of blood that went from the threshold of his door all the way back to a dumpster 250 yards away from his home. The young man had been bleeding from his brachial artery.

Justin was rushed in an ambulance to Moses Cone Memorial Hospital where the doctors and nursed tried everything to bring Justin back, but it was too late. A doctor later told me that if Justin had not fled from where the injury had taken place, he most likely would have lived. Justin's injury, although serious, did not have to be fatal. If the young man could have received some basic level of emergency medical care, there is a high likelihood that Justin would still be living today. It is with great regret and sadness that I must inform you that Justin is buried in a cemetery in Greensboro, North Carolina. All because he chose to run before assessing his wounds.

Much like Justin, your desire at the moment may be to mindlessly flee from the hurt and disappointment in your marriage without seeking treatment for your own hurts and wounds. All you want to do is escape the pain and anguish, but you may aggravate the wound that has already been inflicted. The injury could be fatal to what is left of your marriage, but if someone could offer scriptural guidance, you (and your marriage) would have a chance to survive.

How do we bridge the gap from hopelessness to healing? First, we have to stop the damage caused by words and actions that complicate and aggravate this process. *Marriage Triage* is not a matter of being pragmatic, but "*prayer-matic.*" A part of *Marriage Triage* is taking responsibility for your actions and reactions—without rationalizing away your sinful choices—and avoiding any future sinful choices that could ruin any chance for reconciliation. Emotions can drive us to actions we never imagined. It is important to handle this trial in a way that brings long-term healing as opposed to short-term gratification.

This will not be easy in your current frame of mind, but fortunately the strength doesn't come from you; it comes from Christ alone.

I can do all things through Him [Christ] who strengthens me (Philippians 4:13).

I spent more than a decade as a police officer working in the middle of marital strife and conflict. I will never forget the intensity of the emotions and the way husbands and wives could hurl vicious words (and on some occasions, frying pans) at each other without once considering the impact and permanent nature of their responses. Quite frankly, I heard so much "potty-mouth" throughout those years that I became desensitized to it. When I left law enforcement, it took time, prayer, and years of forming new habits to become re-sensitized after being around foul language and violence for so long. I have seen the kind of cynicism I once possessed in many hurting and broken spouses who have lived through years of pain and disappointment.

Whether a spouse caught their mate with another person or an argument erupted into a physical or emotional confrontation, these situations were in need of immediate intervention. You may wonder what I did as a police officer on many occasions to restore order and peace in those dysfunctional and broken homes. Many times all the police can do is provide an interim answer by taking a spouse to jail or talking someone into leaving for the evening. There was never time to sit down and spend hours helping each spouse learn from their circumstances, and that is outside the realm of police responsibilities, anyway. Such discipleship from a civil servant would most likely be frowned upon. The type of triage I provided was simply an interim fix to survive through the evening until it was time to go off duty. It was a kind of emergency triage that provided no real solution to a cycle of chaos and volatility in the relationship of the couple involved. No real, lasting peace was created other than to hope a spouse would see the need to seek counseling. There was also no guarantee that they would seek any sort of Christian guidance where the heart of the problem could be addressed, as opposed to addressing the symptoms.

You may be a spouse who is familiar with the domestic conflict cycle. Maybe you have experienced the intervention of a police officer in your home. Or, your situation may not be that extreme. Either way, I offer biblical hope for you and your spouse.

DOES YOUR MARRIAGE NEED TRIAGE?

Can I ask you a very direct and honest question? If you had known that marriage could cut, shred, and mince your heart the way that it has, would you have ever gotten married? You probably had an idea of what marriage to the one you love would be like, but you never once imagined yourself betrayed and hurting. It's a lost and debilitating place to be. Trust has been destroyed. Marriage was never supposed to be this way! What went wrong? A marriage built on the solid foundation of Jesus Christ isn't supposed to end up in this place, is it? There will be time for re-assessing your past later, but we must stabilize where you are right now.

If you have a multitude of questions racing through your mind, and your mind is so shell-shocked that it can't formulate even one clear thought, then marriage triage is for you.

YOU DIDN'T CHOOSE THIS SITUATION, BUT YOU HAVE CHOICES

No one comes to this lonely and wretched place by choice or by intentional plan. You didn't end up on this island of pain overnight, and this emotional injury won't heal quickly or swiftly.

You want to know how to proceed, and I am praying that you will be open to responding biblically as opposed to emotionally. You need to take responsibility for your deliberate actions and for your future reactions. I have seen too many spouses take the emotional road and aggravate what is already a volatile and hostile situation.

Marriage triage will help you make biblical choices when your carnal nature wants to rage in retaliation. I know that you feel that your spouse deserves it! You must fight this temptation with a strength that only Jesus Himself can give. You could choose to even the score by going out and duplicating your spouse's sinful actions. If your spouse has been unfaithful, then you might feel justified to do the same thing. If your mate has bankrupted your family, then you think you have every right to finance a brand new car you can't afford. When those feelings rise up, it's time to go back to Jesus' forgiving example. If Jesus can forgive us in spite of our deliberate acts against Him, then we need to choose to give our spouse the same undeserved gesture of love. I am not saying that you should feel like doing this right this very moment. For me to direct you to simply say "I forgive" would be rather naïve on my part. I do want you to be open to the idea of forgiveness as we walk through this valley.

But God demonstrates His own love toward us, in that while we were still sinners, Christ died for us (Romans 5:8).

THE WIFE IN NEED OF TRIAGE

There is a possibility that you are the wife who did it all right. Maybe you were the wife who showed respect and submission in every way, and yet the betrayal still occurred. You took care of the family, submitted, and honored your husband in every possible way, but it didn't stop the adultery. You feel dirty, dishonored, and disheartened. You don't know what step to take or where to go, and it feels life-sucking. I have spoken with wives who could have placed their photographs next to Proverbs 31:10, and yet their marriages still unraveled. A common phrase I hear from wives (and husbands) in my office is "It just isn't fair!" They can't fathom why they must suffer as a result of the sins of the spouse.

There may be so much contention in your spirit toward your husband right now that you have absolutely no clue what to do or who to talk to about your frustrations. Perhaps you've been balancing on that thin line between love and hate. Maybe you found another man who is more attentive to your concerns. Be careful. There are sharks out there just waiting for a shot at your heart, and probably a little more. Even if he's only a male friend with good intentions, you must steer clear and shield your heart. Admittedly, this is a very vulnerable and dangerous place for a married woman to be, especially when you have run from God's plan for marriage. Reading Scriptures such as Ephesians 5:25 may literally turn your stomach and make you want to say things like, "sounds good on a piece of paper, but you don't understand my reality." Maybe you feel that your husband is incapable of loving you this way because of the tattered history the two of you have created. Maybe your husband has never spiritually led you on a consistent basis, and you don't know what a biblical marriage looks like. In fact, one of most common complaints I hear from wives is that their husband refuses to be the spiritual leader of the family. He wants the wife to shoulder it all. Such a dilemma explains where much of the contention arises in a so-called Christian marriage.

With all of this contentiousness present, we must do all we can to minimize the temptation to react emotionally. I am encouraging you to persevere and don't lose heart. The pain is unbearable, but the following chapters will give you a framework to endure through your crisis.

THE HUSBAND IN NEED OF TRIAGE

Maybe you have tried to be a godly husband who mirrors the Bible's definition of a righteous man, and you have still ended up crushed and devastated. Your wife chose to enter into an extramarital affair, and your head is spinning as you brainstorm over what you could have done differently. You thought you had a good marriage. You can't understand what has led you to separation, both physically and emotionally, from your wife. What have you missed? It makes no logical sense! It's as though a concussion grenade just went off in the living room, leaving you lying dazed and confused on the floor.

Perhaps you never took your wife that seriously and never anticipated how emotional she could be. In your reality, she just over-reacted to everything you did or said, and she just needs to get over it! Isn't going to church once a week and coming home every night enough to call what you two have a Christian marriage? You can't understand why your wife just can't let you do what you want and have some freedom and be available for sex when you need it. No one ever sat down and spelled out what a fulfilling biblical marriage was really supposed to be like, so it's not even your fault, right? You may have even faked your way through a few premarital counseling sessions during your engagement, uttering all the right clichés and answers.

The challenge for you is that you will have to step out of your comfort zone no matter what the scenario may be. One of the hardest things I ever did was to seek wise, biblical counsel in my hurt state. In your current state, you need to surround yourself with wise counsel who will point you to biblical answers when your emotions are directing you to pound something. Our reasoning is hard enough when we are in a good state of mind, let alone when your mind is reeling with pain and suffering! You must listen to the Christian counselor who will guide you in a way that honors Christ, even when it makes no sense.

As a former police officer, I have witnessed what a hurt and betrayed husband is capable of doing. Some of those husbands that I dealt with are spending the rest of their lives in prison because of hasty actions that led to death and the lifelong torment of loved ones left behind! You must filter your decisions through a wider lens so that you have some perspective on your choices. When you proceed with the God-honoring perspective, it may not result in reconciliation, but I can guarantee it will most likely not result in justified incarceration!

VIOLENT MARRIAGES

I spent a number of years entering broken and dysfunctional homes, trying to prevent couples from hurting or killing each other. There were always some immediate concerns that had to be addressed before I could even begin to mediate a situation between husband and wife. What you need to determine before going any further is whether you are safe at home. Have you been physically assaulted by your spouse? Are you in a position of continued endangerment? If you have been struck in anger once by your mate, most likely it will occur again. Statistics show that a woman is assaulted or beaten every nine seconds in the US. In fact, I am fairly certain that anyone reading this book who has been assaulted has been struck many times before. In working with abused spouses both as a police officer and as a counselor, I've seen the pattern established. By the time they come to the office, they have been living under a cloud of abuse for a long period of time. If it is your first time, then I applaud you for seeking help sooner rather than later.

If you have been assaulted, your first step is to leave the source of danger and to honor your husband or wife with space. I am not saying to go immediately to divorce court, because God truly hates divorce (Malachi 2:16). At this early stage of the marriage triage assessment, it is necessary for you not to place your spouse in a position to dishonor God any further by abusing you or your children. You can show both submission and honor to your spouse by removing yourself from a position to be harmed by them. God may require you to be submissive, but that can be accomplished by not giving further place to the devil with your presence.

If you are the offending or violent spouse, then I urge you to remove yourself from the volatility immediately! Seek the guidance and help you need in dealing with your violent anger issues. Also, remember that using intimidation tactics to coerce your spouse into anything is just as offensive as physical brutality. Removing yourself could be the difference between jail and freedom. I've lost track of the number of husbands I arrested who may not have intended to hurt their wives, but it happened anyway. Distance yourself, and "man-up" by seeking biblical guidance. (Women are also capable of violence and need to get help to change their destructive behavior.) Getting help and counseling is also a way of showing genuine love for your family. Trash the pride and arrogance, remove yourself, and seek guidance to restore your relationship with your family.

As a former police officer, I encourage an abused spouse to use the court system for legitimate assault(s) and other types of violence. I do not condone any spouse taking a beating or being struck. I urge you to take legal measures to prevent further abuse.

Wives, be subject to your own husbands, as to the Lord (Ephesians 5:22).

And do not give the devil an opportunity (Ephesians 4:27).

Whether you are the husband or the wife, it doesn't change the fact that things have reached some form of critical mass, and you can't take one more minute of it! You have reached the point where your desire to end the pain is overshadowing your love for your spouse. Maybe it's even overshadowing your love for Christ. You likely would agree that you still do love your spouse, but you just don't like him or her anymore. You can't live in this non-communicating world of chaos. You're desperate for some sort of change that doesn't tighten your chest with every thought! You want the indigestible brick in your stomach to just dissolve and for life to have some semblance of normalcy, whatever normalcy may be! Although normalcy cannot be guaranteed, you'll find encouragement and guidance in the following chapters that may be of some assistance—the kind of guidance that you can take to heart so that you can begin your refining journey.

DISCUSSION QUESTIONS

1. Marriage triage is all about immediately addressing the critical areas and preventing impulsive emotional mistakes. What is your biggest emotional temptation at this time? (Examples could be anything from car-keying to confrontation.)

2. How do you plan on controlling the desire to rehash your spouse's sins? What plan can you create to prevent this habit?

3. How do you show honor to an abusive spouse?

4. If your spouse is willing, have him or her read this chapter. Then, discuss it together. Make a list of areas that you both can work through.

INSIGHTS

MARRIAGE TRIAGE

My soul clings to dust; Revive me according to thy word.

~Psalm 119:25

CHAPTER TWO
THE CRISIS BEGINS

RACHEL DIDN'T HAVE A CLUE how to start processing all the information she had learned from her husband, John. Although she knew there had been times of tension and silence throughout their marriage, none of this made any logical sense. John and Rachel were the couple who could not have *issues*, much less fail. They both had positive reputations in their church and were raised by Christian parents. What could possibly have gone wrong?

After being discovered, John had confessed to Rachel that he had been involved in an emotional affair with a mutual family friend and had spent a great deal of time talking and texting with this other woman. Although he knew it was sinful, the other woman gave him attention while Rachel remained focused and busy with all the day-to-day responsibilities of being a working mom and homemaker. Rachel had been so focused on her responsibilities that she had literally lost track of John and his needs in the marriage. As Rachel processed this stunning information, her reeling mind was thrown off-kilter. How should she react? How does she learn to trust, forgive, and move on? Should she move on with or without John? Is her marriage salvageable, or does this cross some impenetrable, one-way boundary that cannot be reversed?

Rachel's emotional side wanted to push away from John—or maybe curl up and hide somewhere in the fetal position. The intense pain and emotional stress she was experiencing made her insides feel heavy and rigid. She was willing to take responsibility for contributing to the framework of this scenario, but she never believed that John could be unfaithful to her, even if it was just emotional and not physical! Or was it? How would she ever really know the truth? Could she trust anything John said ever again? Should she still submit to him, or should she treat him like a diseased leper for the rest of their marriage? Would there still be a marriage?

Rachel didn't want to respond biblically to her circumstances; she wanted to break or destroy something! She wanted to brood over John's offenses and feed her rage. She wanted to remind John every waking moment. She deserved answers to every detailed question about what transpired between John and the other woman! The suggestive e-mails and the text messages between John and the other woman had been surrendered to her. Did she know everything now? Was there undiscovered information that John was failing to disclose? She wanted answers, and she wanted them immediately! She caught herself reading and re-reading the same e-mails and hard copies of the text messages and ruminating over what it all meant. Why did John say those things to this woman? *Does he really love me? Whose face does he see when we make love?* Rachel noticed that her anger climbed higher the more she thought about what had transpired. She wanted to hurt the woman who was interfering in her marriage! She wanted the woman's job, and she wanted the person to feel her hurt and embarrassment! It was becoming easier to overlook her own sins and see only John's and the other woman's. Her humility level decreased while her pride and anger levels increased.

Rachel was at a point where she could no longer focus on any one thing but wanted to escape and run from the source of the pain. She had her bags packed, and she packed a week's worth of clothes and toys for the kids. She gave her parents no details, only telling them that she was coming to visit while John worked on an important project. Rachel was taking care of some last-minute details and had even vacuumed and tidied up the house out of habit. She was just a few feet from the door when she began sobbing uncontrollably. She sent the kids back to their rooms and cried on the couch non-stop for ten minutes. When she regained her composure, she felt like she needed to write a letter to John, but instead she decided to write it to God.

A LETTER TO GOD

Hey God. It's Rachel here, and I am angry, upset, disillusioned, and done. I have some questions for You. How do you rebuild the breach of trust in a marriage? What does it take once infidelity visits the inner sanctum of the mind and then leaves as nonchalantly as it initially entered? What should be my response, oh my Lord? Shall I simply say, "It's okay, I love you, and I know it will be the last time this happens"? Do I rage in anger as the legitimate spouse and demand emotional restitution? God, please tell me what my response should be to the one I love! Should I beat my chest, loathing myself for failing to meet emotional needs of my spouse? Oh God, I need your audible voice to guide my every action! I am so afraid of my own ability to decide the course. If the spouse I love and consider to be more godly than me can fail me and crush my heart, then I can only imagine what I am capable of! Oh Lord, please place Your hand on my heart and let me know You are there! I feel so isolated and emotionally alone.

REACTIONS ARE EVERYTHING?

Where do you go and who do you turn to when your marital reality is exposed as a façade of lies and deceit? Who do you question? From the viewpoint of the world, you have every right to "kick them to the curb," but is that a biblical response? Is it one strike and out you go? What do you do? You have been forcefully placed in a position to make critical decisions about your marriage. The problem is you may not have a Ph.D. in marital problem solving.

This book, although not exhaustive, will focus on the critical moment when you received the devastating revelation that your marriage is in trouble. Maybe your spouse has gone out and spent your life savings, or you may be a spouse who has been betrayed—or you may be an adulterer whose sin has been exposed. What are you going to do now? Will you respond biblically or emotionally? I understand it is too early to throw out the "just forgive them" language. You are in immense pain and need guidance and encouragement. You need someone trustworthy to tell you that you can make it, no matter what the outcome may be!

My goal is to help you stop any further damage while dealing with crucial decisions about the future of your marriage. The Bible is our source for help; God's Word will guide us to make the right choices for our families. Even if you do not profess to be a believer, I am asking you to read and consider the claims I will make throughout this book. Maybe you have tried many other ways to address your pain, and you are desperate. The biblical standards you need to apply to your situation may seem a very illogical if you compare them to pop culture. The lessons we need to learn are not in any way egocentric. They are Christ-centric. Jesus told us if anyone desires to come after Him, they must first deny themselves. Such an approach goes contrary to what the world demands, especially when it comes to personal relationships.

And He was saying to them all, "If anyone wishes to come after Me, he must deny himself, and take up his cross daily and follow me (Luke 9:23).

The way we learn to follow Jesus is a daily process, not a one-time event. Get ready to start a day-by-day process of evaluating and re-evaluating your situations and circumstances. In the climax of distress, it is easy to focus on one particular moment in time when it is more important to see the big picture. You will have days where it feels like the walls are crumbling, but you must not lose heart!

Therefore we do not lose heart, but though our outer man is decaying, yet our inner man is being renewed day by day (2 Corinthians 4:16).

FIRST RESPONDER

As a police officer, I was required to attend First Responder classes where we were taught how to give aid to people in the midst of a medical emergency. All of these classes were geared toward teaching us how to isolate, slow down, and minimize the injuries the victim had received. The wounds may have been inflicted by an assailant or even by the victims themselves. No two injuries were exactly the same, but that didn't change the primary goal of the encounter, which was to get the bleeding stopped and insure the medical situation didn't get worse. In many cases, such actions turned out to be the difference between life and death. If you can grasp this simple principle, then much of what you read will be easier to synthesize into useful information. You are learning how to stabilize any emotional injuries that exist in your marriage.

FAITHFUL TO THE END, BEGINNING OR RENEWAL

Even though we know that God can do anything, our free will comes into play in our marital relationships. If a spouse walks out of the marriage, there is always the possibility that restoration will never occur. We must understand that our acts of obedience to God don't always result in what we want. We want our marriage restored! We want to forget all that has transpired! We want simple love and romance without the complications! If these are our goals, we will easily become disillusioned with our circumstances. Sometimes our only earthly reward comes from knowing we are faithful to Christ. It means that we strive for obedience that will make us content even when we don't feel happy.

Not that I speak from want; for I have learned to be content in whatever circumstances I am (Philippians 4:11).

JOHN AND RACHEL

Rachel felt rather lifeless and confused, but it wasn't her desire to give up on her marriage. The pain was intense, but Rachel wanted to find a way to center the marriage back where it was supposed to be.

Even though John felt the same way, it didn't remove the wounded and lifeless feelings. Rachel would frequently catch her mind drifting and dwelling on John's actions and getting herself all knotted up inside. John dreaded coming to bed some nights because he was so tired of rehashing his sinful actions and insisting in the face of Rachel's disbelief that it had never reached the physical stage. Rachel would even begin questioning John's sincerity because he wasn't acting as emotional as she was. The irony of the situation was that Rachel's actions were just as sinful. Her dwelling and rehashing continued to leave the wounds wide open. Healing was not being allowed to happen. She came under a great deal of conviction one particular night as she read from Proverbs. In fact, it was the first time she had been consistently reading her Bible in years.

A worthless man digs up evil, while his words are like scorching fire (Proverbs 16:27).

When Rachel read this, she felt as though God was pointing a finger directly at her! She had been so interested in uncovering secrets that she lost track of her responsibilities as John's wife. She wept bitter tears realizing that interrogating John was doing nothing but stirring up evil and throwing John's past wrongs in his face while subjecting herself to more emotional agony.

John knew he had violated every bit of trust Rachel deeply cherished, but he didn't want to leave the relationship. He wanted to prove to Rachel his sorrow for his actions.

Rachel began realizing through her own pain that she had a precious healing gift to offer John that no other woman on the planet could administer. As the betrayed one, she had the ability to offer forgiveness to John. Rachel began to realize that just as Christ alone forgave her sins, Rachel could do the same for John in their marriage. It's not that John deserved to be forgiven, but her pain helped her to see that she had no right to forgiveness, either. They were both sinners who had received the gift of forgiveness from their heavenly Father years before they ever were married.

But God demonstrates His own love toward us, in that while we were still sinners, Christ died for us (Romans 5:8).

Rachel accepted that this process was going to take a great deal of time and intentional energy; there are no shortcuts to emotional healing. As much as both Rachel and John had a desire to be renewed, neither had a clue where to begin. In this early stage of their crisis, there were many loose ends to tie off and protective measures to take. They needed to be sure that all the wounds that led them to this dark time in their marriage were stabilized and cauterized. Rachel was thankful that as bad as things were right now, they weren't as bad as they could have been. There were many married couples in much worse shape. John had the desire to rebuild and learn from his sins, where some erring spouses don't. He desired forgiveness from Rachel, and Rachel desired to be what God wanted her to be in their marriage. They were willing to learn how to function in unity and forgiveness together.

The issue that caused them the most pain at this stage was the open wounds left from emotional hurt and feelings of betrayal. Rachel still doubted that John had told her everything, and she needed guidance in dealing with her emotions. They both began to sense the need of finding godly counsel to help guide them through this struggle in their marriage. It required a person who could help them biblically and hold them accountable for the actions they needed to take in order to restore their marriage to what God intended it to be. What both John and Rachel began to realize is that their goal wasn't to restore what they had, but to strive for something in their marriage they had never before possessed—a truly unified front with Christ in the center of every thought and decision.

DISCUSSION QUESTIONS

1. If you are in the middle of an emotional crisis in your marriage, what should you do first to help prevent yourself from overreacting emotionally? List some ways spouses may overreact emotionally.

2. Based on this chapter, what have you learned about forgiveness? Is forgiveness a quick process, or does it take time and commitment?

3. Discuss what you would do if you were John. What actions can John take to show his sincerity?

4. Discuss what you would do if you were Rachel. Would you be willing to make a commitment to forgive even if you didn't "feel" like it?

INSIGHTS

MARRIAGE TRIAGE

God's Grace Never Leaves

Own Your Sins and Failures

Document Your Thoughts and Experiences

Counsel with Godly People

Adapt To Your Circumstances

Respond Biblically

Endure Through Your Circumstances

Shield Your Heart

And the Law came in that the transgression might increase; but where sin increased, grace abounded all the more.

~Romans 5:20

CHAPTER THREE

GOD'S GRACE NEVER LEAVES

Is there ever a time you feel less grace-filled than others? Maybe a better way to ask this question would be to inquire if your spouse ever deserved less grace than what you are showing them now in the midst of conflict. I don't have to know the details of your marriage crisis to know that, in the eyes of the world, any kind gestures shown to your spouse may not be deserved.

SPEEDING FROM GRACE

I used to love to work traffic enforcement as a police officer. I know it sounds awful to the typical citizen, but I found it to be a lot of fun. Maybe it was the thrill of the chase or the skill of using the K-55 radar, but there was a little rush an officer received from working traffic! In fact, I will share a little inside information with you on how an officer can write tickets without any sense of emotion, something that I learned from my instructor, Clyde Elkins, in the police academy. There are basically two kinds of drivers in this world: the caught and the un-caught. Much like the wording of Romans 3:23, all officers understood that "all have sped and deserve a speeding ticket." Have

I gotten your face all good and red yet? As the one writing this, I'm certainly blushing!

I recall stopping a soccer mom for speeding in a newer model mini-van, and she had the audacity to ask me a ridiculous question. She asked me if I had met my "quota" for the day. Being a highly trained and quick-witted officer, I immediately replied, "To be honest, ma'am, you just got my wife a new toaster. Thank you very much!" I rode around the rest of the shift just waiting to get called into my sergeant's office for being disrespectful to the public. (For the record, my instructor taught me that saying too.)

The truth is that we all fall short of deserving grace, but we all have an overwhelming desire to receive the gift of grace. None of the people I cited for speeding desired to be treated fairly; they preferred to be treated with grace! Furthermore, there are people in your life who assuredly don't deserve to be treated fairly or justly in your eyes. They deserve a swift kick in the seat, you think to yourself, but is this the correct response according to God's Word?

When you have been betrayed and deceived, it is easy to become a person who desires to uphold the "rule of law." If your spouse has been unfaithful, irresponsible, or even dishonest, then why should grace even come into the picture? Stop and think it over. Is grace really an undeserved and unearned gift, or do the rules change when your spouse sins?

DO YOU LOVE CHRIST LESS WHEN YOUR WORLD FALLS APART?

When we talk about grace, we may sometimes be tempted to place some sort of controlled measure of how much grace we give at a time. The problem with such a system is that Christ never placed any limits on His grace and love toward us. Christ went so far as to do His part without any guarantee that any of us would ever reciprocate the gesture.

But God demonstrates His own love toward us, in that while we were yet sinners, Christ died for us (Romans 5:8).

Jesus willingly and purposefully gave His life for us on the cross without one smidgen of a promise that we would ever commit our hearts and lives to Him. We call this a unilateral gesture. Jesus took one lash after the other and allowed his creation to crucify Him because He loved you and me! When we begin to think that we can limit the grace and mercy we show others, all we have to do is remember the cross of Calvary in order to get the right perspective. No one deserves the grace of Christ, and yet He gave us grace upon grace!

For by grace you have been saved through faith; and that not of yourselves, it is the gift of God; not as a result of works, that no one should boast (Ephesians 2:8-9).

The predicament of many disillusioned spouses is that they can be tempted to love Christ less in their trials. We measure how much we love Jesus by what He has done for us *lately* instead of what He already did on our behalf. He saved us from eternal separation and hell, and yet we are more concerned with the here and now. We quickly forget how undeserving we are of His matchless grace and are more concerned with the way we have been offended and betrayed.

You may think I am minimizing the anguish you are feeling, but I simply want you to see your circumstances in a bigger frame. God's grace hasn't disrupted its flow to your life, I promise! It's too easy to forget that it's still there being abundantly poured out, even in the peak of your suffering. I can attest to times of feeling like the walls were caving in, and my world seemed so much smaller. My list of worries had shortened to nothing but my own hurts, pain, and sorrow. I couldn't recall prayer requests for any other human soul on the planet. I couldn't motivate myself to eat or sleep; when I tried, I would just dwell and relive my pain. Grace wasn't real high on my priority list because I couldn't gather up the energy to make the list. I just wanted to stay parked on hurting, dwelling, and anger. It's not that it was by any stretch of the imagination working for me, but I wanted it to be all about me.

Why Should You Demonstrate Grace?

When we have reached the point where we are literally immobilized by our pain and anger, we must pull out a new strategy for dealing with the problem. This is the place where we must understand that we signed up as a child of God for life, and Christ requires our obedience and loyalty. This loyalty and love means that when we don't feel like obeying, we obey anyway.

If you love Me, you will keep My commandments (John 14:15).

GRACE GOES HAND-IN-HAND WITH FORGIVENESS

If you have been within a football field's length of a church, you have heard grace described as the unmerited (undeserved) favor of God. Grace is "God's loving mercy toward mankind[3]." Another way it is described is "grace involves such other subjects as forgiveness, salvation, regeneration, repentance and the love of God[4]." Maybe you had a more limited view of grace before now, but grace covers just about every area we will discuss in subsequent pages.

Part of God's love for us emanates in the perfect and holy way He forgives us despite all our imperfections and frailties. When we grasp the way God's grace works in our lives, we begin to see that there is hope even when we can't see the future in our marriage. When we hurt and suffer from betrayal and deception, we can easily lose our ability to forgive because we don't see the purpose or the need. In fact, there may be moments the only reason you demonstrate grace and forgiveness is out of obedience to Christ. Christ doesn't ask us to *feel* like being obedient; He just requires our obedience, regardless of our emotions. It also means that we must sometimes pledge to forgive our spouse while God works to bring equality in both our emotions and commitment.

WHY SHOULD I DEMONSTRATE GRACE AND FORGIVENESS?

There have been numerous individuals who have asked me if they must forgive their spouse even if their spouse isn't remorseful. I have heard countless stories of spouses who have run off to pursue other relationships, leaving the betrayed spouse in shock and dismay. Some, while spending away the family savings, have unrepentantly refused to break off contact with the partner in adultery. Are these exceptions to the rule because they want no forgiveness? Is there a breakpoint where forgiveness and grace are null and void? I must admit there have been moments I was tired of watching a grieving individual being shredded inside by a selfish and self-centered sorry excuse of a spouse, but it my role didn't allow me to make an exception clause. The Bible gives no exclusions on forgiveness. Even when a relationship ends in divorce, there must be total forgiveness in order to be obedient to Christ and to be an effective witness. The Bible commands it.

For if you forgive men for their transgressions, your heavenly Father will also forgive you (Matthew 6:14-15).

Then Peter came and said to Him, "Lord, how often shall my brother sin against me and I forgive him? Up to seven times?" Jesus said to him, "I do not say to you, up to seven times, but up to seventy times seven" (Matthew 18:21-22).

You can choose to forgive and demonstrate grace in your crisis, knowing that you are exercising obedience to God in the face of adversity. You can also choose to simply let your lack of forgiveness build, grow, and fester. There is nothing more disheartening than an individual who has chosen to hang onto anger and bitterness, believing this refusal to forgive somehow hurts the guilty spouse, but it doesn't. It's like drinking poison and expecting the enemy to die. In fact, everyone but the offending spouse suffers from such a spirit. That unforgiving spirit is just as sinful as the offenses of the guilty spouse.

MERCY AND JUDGMENT

As a child, I made a habit out of talking back to my mother. At times she would spank me, and other times she would make me read as a form of punishment. Of all the things she made me read, the book of James was the most effective. As I entered my teens, I continued to read James quite regularly. There are probably noted theologians who have read and studied this book far less than I. You could say I was a fourteen-year-old subject-matter expert on James. As you can probably guess, I was also a slow learner because you would think that I was practicing all that I learned, but I wasn't. However, there are some key lessons I took from James through the years, lessons on the topics of mercy, the tongue, and judgment.

For judgment will be merciless to one who has shown no mercy; mercy triumphs over judgment. (James 2:13).

No matter how much you have been offended, you cannot hold onto it and remain healthy. In order for you to heal through your suffering, you must allow mercy, grace, and forgiveness to flow freely. Only then can you reach a place of resolve and contentment in your life. Other family members may depend on you emotionally and spiritually, and they need to see you demonstrate a true Christ-likeness. Don't lose heart or hope in your circumstances! Know that no matter what the offense may be, God can give you the strength and resolve to forgive and to show grace to your spouse.

WHAT WE TRULY DESERVE

Let's talk briefly from a Christian perspective about what we truly deserve in this life. We came into this world as sinners guilty before a holy God (Romans 3:23). If you don't believe me, then review the Ten Commandments. You will discover that you have violated more than one of them (Exodus 20). As this is the case, there is a price you will pay for your sinful condition, and that price is death (Romans 6:23). There is also an invitation to receive a gift that God has made available to us all, demonstrated in the form of His Son Jesus. Without the atoning death of Jesus, there would be no way for us to bridge the gap between our sin and a holy God. Jesus is the Son of God, second person in the Trinity, born of a virgin. He was both fully God and fully man when He arrived on earth as a baby. He lived a sinless life and ministered as noted throughout the Gospels, both teaching God's truth and performing miracles. He offered up himself on the cross to provide a "once and for all" sacrifice and to atone for our sins! Christ made a way for us to have fellowship with the Father (2 Corinthians 5:21). As much as Christ did this "once and for all" work on the cross, it is a gift that we must claim for ourselves. I can place a Ferrari in your driveway and leave the keys in the ignition, but until you sit in the driver's seat and turn the key, it is of no use to you. Can you begin to imagine all of the people in the world who will never accept the gift Jesus has freely offered to them? Billions in the world will never accept what Jesus has done for them through His "once and for all" atoning gift on the cross. Instead, many will spend their entire lives embittered to temporal demands of rights, money, and entitlements.

JOHN AND RACHEL

On the same night that John told Rachel the story of his past sins, Rachel made a resolute and unwavering decision. It wasn't the kind of decision that could be made flippantly. Such a decision would require her to stay committed when her emotions were driving her to seek revenge and restitution. Could she really abide by such a decision, knowing there would be moments she wanted to change her mind? Maybe if she placed some stipulations on her decision, it would seem more logical. No, her decision could only be made with no strings attached and without an expectation of reciprocity. To offer forgiveness is to give a gift without seeking one in return. It had to be freely and completely unconditional. Her decision had nothing to do with John. Her decision was grounded in her desire to obey Christ. If her decision was based solely on John, she would have left the relationship and fled from the pain that same evening.

Rachel committed to John that she would strive to forgive him and that she desired for them to work through the hurt and betrayal. Although she knew they were in for some long nights and days, she was committed to learning how to offer unconditional forgiveness.

Such a commitment didn't mean she would do it all the right way, but she would strive to act biblically regardless of her hurt and emotions. She was willing to take any steps necessary to restore their marriage and honor Christ. John was deeply humbled by Rachel's offer, but he also knew that it would take some time for the healing to begin. He knew there would be days when Rachel didn't feel forgiving, but commitment is not to be driven by feelings. They both had to accept that they would have ups and downs while trying to forget the past and press toward the future. Their commitment to Christ had to overshadow the circumstances in their marriage continually.

DISCUSSION QUESTIONS

1. What do you typically do when your world falls apart? Do you begin blaming? Do you question God?

2. Is it ever okay to continue throwing your spouse's sins or past wrongs in his or her face? What are some ways to practice grace and resist the temptation of rehashing past sins?

3. Discuss what Proverbs 16:27 means and how it applies to your situation.

4. Describe ways you can show mercy and grace to an unrepentant spouse.

INSIGHTS

MARRIAGE TRIAGE

God's Grace Never Leaves

Own Your Sins and Failures

Document Your Thoughts and Experiences

Counsel with Godly People

Adapt To Your Circumstances

Respond Biblically

Endure Through Your Circumstances

Shield Your Heart

But He gives a greater grace. Therefore it says, "God opposed the proud, but gives grace to the humble."
~James 4:6

God has given us the "right" to sin, but He has given us the "privilege" to obey (not sin).
~Steve Goode

CHAPTER FOUR
OWN YOUR SINS AND FAILURES

God has given us the "right" to sin, but He has given us the "privilege" to obey (not sin).

I WOULD LIKE TO SHARE a big secret with you about what makes my day as a biblical counselor. There are occasions when people march into my office, look me dead in the eye, and say, "This is my entire fault! No matter what my spouse says, I own the biggest part of the blame for what has occurred!" When I hear these words, I want to do the "Snoopy dance" all the way down the office hallway and back. It energizes me to know that I have a fully engaged, humble counselee, and I look forward to beginning the recovery process with that individual! I am empathetic for what the counselee had to go through to reach this place of humility, but I rejoice that this individual is now a moldable piece of clay in the Master's hands.

The antithesis of the humble counselee is the spouse who enters my doors with a job for me to perform. To that person, I am a marriage mechanic, and my job is to "fix" the other spouse. This one is a totally innocent little lamb married to the devil—or she-devil in certain cases.

Many spouses have brought one another into a mindset of no humility through a slow and arduous process of humility blasting. Unfortunately, until both find their humility, it is difficult for either to see their own mistakes and failures. Many of the spouses who enter my office have no support from their mate and are having to carry on in their lives with a spouse who won't acknowledge their wrongs.

MY SPOUSE MADE ME THIS WAY

A common assertion I hear from husbands and wives is that their spouse is the reason that they act a certain way (sin). To paraphrase it, they are saying, "This isn't the person that I am. It's just who I become when I am with my spouse."

Such an assumption is nothing more than blame-shifting. If you are a Christian, you will one day stand before the Father and give an account for your life. When this moment comes, you will not be able to blame your sins and failures on anyone. You stand alone having only Jesus to cover your sins in his righteousness. You are not defined by your spouse but by your Savior Jesus Christ! You stand alone and are responsible for everything you've done. If you are a genuine believer, then you are in Christ.

For the love of Christ controls us, having concluded this, that one died for all, therefore all died; and He died for all, that they who live should no longer live for themselves, but for Him who died and rose again on their behalf (2 Corinthians 5:14-15).

Therefore if any man is in Christ, he is a new creature; the old things passed away; behold, new things have come (2 Corinthians 5:17).

A common occurrence is the wife who comes to my office in a state of bitterness that is discernible to everyone around. The eye rolling, the scowls, and the contention are engrained responses to her husband. You may think I side with the wife in all these cases. I understand completely how the wife arrived at that wretched place. Wives desire to be spiritually led, cared for, and cherished. When the husband doesn't supply these biblical needs, the wife becomes frustrated, lonely, and embittered. The problem we must solve is how the wife can avoid becoming just as sinful as her husband from the responses she chooses. Yes, I understand why the wife responses the way she does, but that doesn't make it acceptable to God.

See to it that no one comes short of the grace of God; that no root of bitterness springing up causes trouble, and by it many be defiled (Hebrews 12:15).

For a bitter wife or husband, who will be defiled by your bitterness? The passage says many can be defiled by our bitterness and contention. Let me clue you in on who may be impacted. Your children, family, and friends will be contaminated by your bitter spirit. As a biblical counselor, I find that bitterness is one of the hardest mindsets to root out of a husband or wife. It can't be reasoned with, it looks for faults, and it is blind to its own weaknesses. I would even assert that the only place bitterness belongs is in a good cup of strong coffee.

The bitter spouse is more likely to verbally bash the other one, both in and out of that one's presence. The bitter spouse will be sure that all those around know just how inadequate the other spouse is. The children of the bitter spouse will be negatively impacted by such behavior. It creates an atmosphere of uncertainty and edginess that makes both children and adults anxious.

THE DEVIL MADE ME DO IT!

In 2010 I was interviewed about an old murder case that occurred twenty years earlier in Greensboro, NC. The series being filmed was called *The Devil You Know*, and the episode was named "Devil of a Dad." To date, the series has made its rounds on a number of noted networks, including Discovery ID. The case involved a man named Tim Boczkowski who murdered his wife Elaine in the bathtub of their apartment while their three children were in the house. Due to some complications in the case, no murder charges could be filed in Greensboro. Tim Boczkowski moved his kids to Pennsylvania, where he married a woman named Maryann. Tim's son Todd later commented that the striking similarities between his real mom (Elaine) and his stepmom (Maryann) were a comfort to him. Tim's children grew very close to Maryann.

In 1995 Tim Boczkowski killed Maryann in their recently purchased Jacuzzi. Boczkowski's actions led to him being convicted of the murder of both his first wife, Elaine, and his second wife, Maryann. Tim's current residence is in a North Carolina Correctional Institution, where he is serving a life sentence for the murder of his first wife, Elaine.[8]

In 2010 I traveled to Greensboro to film the interview with a media company out of Canada. The interview took hours, and I had to uncover memories of a case that I had not dwelled on for more than fourteen years. One of the questions I was asked had to do with evil. The interviewer asked me if I thought Timothy Boczkowski was an evil person. I pondered for a moment and said, "The Bible says that the heart of man is wicked and evil and cannot be tamed by anyone but God (Jeremiah 17:9). This means that apart from the presence of God in our life, we are capable of any evil act."

We have this big misconception that the presence of the devil is what causes our evil, but it's actually the absence of the presence of God. Your spouse cannot make you act differently, but when you refuse to acknowledge Christ, you will act in an evil manner.

The heart is more deceitful than all else and is desperately sick; who can understand it (Jeremiah 17:9)?

HUMILITY

Humility is defined as a humble condition or attitude of mind. The Oxford dictionary wastes little time in defining the word—it is almost self-explanatory. It's the characteristic of a person who doesn't have an inflated ego or embellished sense of importance. It's the type of person people want to be around because that individual is most likely "real," as opposed to pretentious.

A person with all humility doesn't mind acknowledging the flaws and kinks in his or her life. When things fall apart, we never hear that one say "not my fault!" Humility is the quality of not knowing everything and being okay with not knowing.

Humility can sometimes mean that you must strive to be the person God desires for you to emulate in the marriage even when there is no reward. To put it another way, God has called you to be the right person even when it seems you have married the wrong person.

YOU MARRIED THE WRONG PERSON

I once heard a pastor discuss the topic of spouses who think that they married the wrong person. The pastor explained how some people use this type of phrase to justify many of their feelings and actions. It's an easy way to pin the blame on the other spouse and ignore one's own part of the relationship. I personally have lost count of the number of spouses who have used similar phrases to describe the feelings they have toward their mates when it appears the love has been lost, betrayed, or damaged.

I recall speaking with a husband who felt that he had married outside of God's will. He reached this conclusion because his wife, who had no zeal for spiritual matters, had unremorsefully entered into an affair with another man. One Christian relationship after another has entered into a disillusioned state because of intense hurt, pain, loneliness, and selfishness on the part of one or both spouses who have become too impatient to wait on an answer from God in their marital relationship. They have reached the point where they simply conclude that they must have married the wrong person.

Before I address the question of whether a believer *can* marry the wrong person, I want to discuss the actions of a person who may have reached this conclusion. If a spouse is fixed on believing that he or she married the wrong person, then it stands to reason that the right person must be out there waiting. Whether in actual words or actions, this spouse has also concluded that it is perfectly acceptable to continue treating the other spouse as the wrong person since the marriage was obviously a mistake. A spouse with this mindset is in an extremely vulnerable position, because I can assure you that the counterfeit Mister or Miss Right is out there waiting for a shot! It's that person with the listening ear who claims to know just how you feel. It's that person with whom you are convinced you can be deeper than your spouse because this one knows and accepts you as you are and makes you feel so good about yourself. Before you know it, you are treating this stranger in your life as the right person and shoving your mate to the curb as the wrong person. The truth is that the new Mister or Miss Right doesn't know you better at all.

In her book, *I Do Again*5, Cheryl Scruggs concludes that in emotional affairs the strangers always win because they know only the good side and don't see you in the confines of your own home. They are safe because you can choose what you want them to know and leave out the weaknesses. You can simply live day to day in the "drug-like" euphoria of the moment and become addicted to feelings and experiences with the so-called stranger. I like referring to this state of mind as "counterfeit contentment" because although it looks and feels real, deep down it's all a façade of deceit and betrayal. The Bible says that it is a dangerous infatuation when feelings grow faster than our commitment (Song of Solomon 2:7).

We have now returned to the important but difficult question of whether a Christian can marry the wrong person. According to the Bible, a man will leave his father and mother and be joined to his wife, and they will become one flesh (Genesis 2:24). As we continue through the Bible, we see numerous illustrations of the importance of permanent or lasting marriages. Jesus told us in Matthew that marriage is a permanent union between man and woman (Matthew 19:6). We see examples of where, although Abigail married David, she did not do so until after her husband died (1 Samuel 25). Another powerful story is found in the book of Esther, where Esther was married to the king and was lonely and miserable. She had not seen her husband for weeks when her cousin, Mordecai, encouraged her. He told her that she had been placed in this royal marriage and had a great purpose for such a time as this (Esther 4:14; Romans 8:28).

My answer to this question is that whether you have married the wrong person or the right person is totally irrelevant! It doesn't matter if you married the right or wrong person because God has called you to *be* the right person!

In your marriage, God has placed a call on you to obey Him and all the plans He has for you. Your purpose in your marriage is to strive toward obedience to God, regardless of how you feel.

My wife April and I can testify that there were mornings we awoke in our marriage when we felt lonely and miserable, and the only motivation we had was obedience to Christ. Someone reading this article may be there today. Maybe you imagine yourself married to someone else, or you just tired of being unhappy in your marriage. You will not find a single Scripture that commands you to be happy (or promises that you will be happy) in your marriage, but there are plenty of passages that call you to honor your commitment—also known as your marriage covenant! Even when you can't see the purpose in returning or staying in what seems to be a miserable marriage, God is strong and firm in his purpose for you. He has placed you in your marriage (kids or no kids) for such a time and purpose as this.

Don't give up on the covenant you made with God to remain faithful to your spouse. Understand that, through your successes and failures in your marriage, God desires your obedience to Him. If you have lost the "feelings" for your husband or wife, then pray that God would restore those feelings. The key is a desire to be obedient to him first and then to wait patiently for the feelings to be restored by God, not by anything you can do.

Aren't you glad that as the bride of Christ, we have never been abandoned after all of our many failures and affairs? Christ has loved us through some of the craziest behavior one could ever imagine, and yet he hasn't left us for a person who seemed more right. The Bible says that God commended His love to us in that while we were active in our sin, he still gave his life for us (Romans 5:8). Jesus didn't enjoy being beaten by cruel men and hung on a cross to suffer until dead, but he did it anyway. He showed us a level of commitment that has a permanent and unconditional meaning.

To wives and husbands with unloving spouses, I offer you my sympathy, but I offer no get–out-of-marriage-free card (Matthew 19:6). God has placed you where you are, whether wrong or right, to be the right person and to be obedient to God. God will provide the contentment you need and will sustain you because of your obedience (Philippians 4:11).

THE SIN OF DWELLING

Dwelling is one of the easiest things to do when your heart is broken. You want to wallow in your grief and relive all the betrayal and hurt. Or maybe you don't want to, but your brain won't shut down and let you escape the memories. Maybe there is one specific moment that something was said that you just can't let go of. Dwelling on it can keep you in an anxious state of mind that leaves you unfocused and unable to accomplish the simplest of tasks. In an article a number of years ago, I discussed anxiousness in the context of where we need to allow our minds to dwell. Dwelling and ruminating on circumstances in our lives can lead us into a dark and lonely place. Dwelling is not interested in a solution as much as it is in focusing on our own worry. The reason the Bible calls worry a sin is that it's the jumping point for a number of hopeless locations.

DEALING WITH WORRY IN OUR LIVES

Worry is the chronic or even occasional act of dwelling on our negative actions and circumstances with no confidence that a solution will ever be revealed. Worry reveals a lack of faith. I believe we can all relate to this type of worry and anxiousness. It's the kind that makes your stomach feel slightly knotted with just a dash of increased heartbeat. Once you have reached this level of worry, it's hard to focus on anything else! Maybe you are dwelling on how to pay the bills, your relationship to your spouse, or some other negative or uncontrollable circumstances. It could be that you are caught up in dwelling on past mistakes, and you just can't shake the flashbacks! Let me be the first to confess that I have traveled down most of these dwelling roads, and it's not pleasant. There are even times we can feel situational feelings of depression over what we let our minds dwell on. Sometimes the symptoms of worry can be so emotionally painful that you're tempted to get a prescription, thinking it will fix your anxiousness. Take my word for it, unless you have a true chemical condition, it won't work. There are no magic pills.

Now that I have gotten you good and depressed, you probably feel anxious about where this discussion is headed. We have learned that we arrived at a bad place because we focused our thoughts on the wrong things, which is not biblical. The Bible tells us to fix our thoughts on honorable and true things. Christ desires for us to spend time on things that are worthy of praise.

Finally brethren, whatever is true, whatever is honorable, whatever is right, whatever is pure, whatever is lovely, whatever is of good repute, if there is any excellence and if anything worthy of praise, dwell on these things (Philippians 4:8).

The problem was never simply fixing our mind, but fixing it on the wrong things! Quiz yourself and see where you have been allowing your mind to dwell. Can you honestly say it was fixated on pure and honorable things?

We need to understand that to worry is a sin! The Bible says that we are to worry or be anxious for nothing (Philippians 4:6). Paul goes on to tell us that we are to pray and give thanks to God because he is the ultimate peace giver! The result of bathing your issues in prayer is that God will guard your heart. Wow, we can be protected and guarded by God where we can be hurt the most, our heart. We are also specifically told to cast all of our cares on Him because He cares for us (1 Peter 5:7). As we go down the list of Scriptures, we begin to lose traction on our excuse-paved worry road.

Dwelling appears to play a major role in building anxiety, so let's talk for a moment about better areas to allow our minds to linger. Is there a place for a Christian's mind to dwell where it can feel completely and totally safe from the circumstances and hurt of this world? I discovered the answer to this from an elderly gentleman that my wife April and I used to help care for.

His name was Roy Harris. He was a ninety-year-old homebound Alzheimer's patient. Each time we would go by to see him, we would ask him to recite Psalm 91. You see, even though Roy was in the latter stages of Alzheimer's, he had memorized Psalm 91 when he was younger, and even through all he had forgotten, that Psalm still dwelled in his mind. The first verse of the passage says "He that dwelleth in the secret place of the most High shall abide under the shadow of the Almighty" (Psalm 91:1 KJV).

I learned a great deal from Roy about where my mind needs to dwell when I want genuine peace and contentment. I can dwell in the very presence of the Almighty God! I do this by spending extended time in reading the Bible and in prayer. There is no better way to rid my body of the feelings of worry and anxiousness! Think about this: Jesus Christ was subjected to the very same temptations, worry, and anxiety that we each face every day. The Bible says that Jesus experienced all of these emotions while on earth. Jesus understands and cares deeply for us and where we are in our lives.

For we do not have a high priest who cannot sympathize with our weaknesses, but One who has been tempted in all things as we are, yet without sin. Therefore let us draw near with confidence to the throne of grace, so that we may receive mercy and find grace to help in time of need (Hebrews 4:15-16).

Where has your mind been dwelling? Have you been worried and anxious about many things in and around you? It's so easy to let your mind dwell in the negative with your marriage's uncertain future. My prayers are with all those who have allowed worry and anxiety to encompass their lives. I pray that you will dwell in the shelter of the Most High today.

DISCUSSION QUESTIONS

1. What is your greatest area of worry regarding your marriage?

2. What is the most difficult part of being the right person in your marriage?

3. Read Ephesians 5:22-33 and write down what God requires of you as a spouse.

4. Look up the word covenant in a dictionary and discuss it in terms of your marriage.

INSIGHTS

MARRIAGE TRIAGE

God's Grace Never Leaves

Own Your Sins and Failures

Document Your Thoughts and Experiences

Counsel with Godly People

Adapt To Your Circumstances

Respond Biblically

Endure Through Your Circumstances

Shield Your Heart

But the Helper, the Holy Spirit, whom the Father will send in My name, He will teach you all things, and bring to remembrance all that I said to you.

~John 14:26

CHAPTER FIVE

DOCUMENT YOUR THOUGHTS AND EXPERIENCES

WE DO OUR BEST WRITING and journaling when we are in the midst of great pain and emotional suffering. As ironic as it seems, there is something special about these moments in our life that opens up a new discernment that lasts for the duration of the pain before ebbing away in a slow process of healing.

I WEAR MY SUNGLASSES AT NIGHT

Police officers commonly respond to burglary calls in the dark of night. The biggest problem with nighttime responses is figuring out how to get to the scene of the crime both quickly and stealthily. A little trick I was taught by a training officer was to wear sunglasses on the way to the burglary call. I always carried a nice pair of "Raybangs" that I purchased at a local convenience mart for around four dollars. Despite the fact that they made the top of my ear break out on occasion, they were a good pair of cheap knock-off sunglasses.

The reason for wearing sunglasses to a nighttime alarm call had nothing to do with being cool. As I drove through the dark wearing sunglasses, my eyes were slowly adjusting to the lack of illumination. By the time I arrived at the site of the burglary, my eyes were accustomed to seeing in the darkness. I would then take the sunglasses off, and my night vision was optimized.

The reason that you can see things others cannot is because you have adjusted to being in your own emotional darkness. You are temporarily more sensitive to the hurts and pains of those around you. For this reason, it will be important for you to journal and write down your experiences before this new vision adjusts to the light. Take advantage of this feature so that you can read it with a reflective perspective later on when the time is right.

You will also notice that as you read Scriptures, they will come to life in a whole new way because of your hurt and suffering. There are Scripture passages that bring tears to my eyes even today because of all the experiences God brought me through.

The Lord is our refuge and strength, a very present help in trouble (Psalm 46:1).

He who dwells in the shelter of the Most High will abide in the shadow of the Almighty (Psalm 91:1).

I will lift up my eyes to the mountains; From whence shall my help come? My help comes from the Lord, Who made heaven and earth (Psalm 121:1-2).

To the person who has never endured real pain, these Scriptures may seem meaningful, but to those who have been brought to their knees, such passages are lifelines to the Father! When our circumstances are uncertain, we are in a position to choose where our faith lies. It either lies in God's abundant mercy or our own efforts.

OLD JOURNALS OF MINE

I have been keeping journals in some form for the past fifteen years. I remember dusting one of those journals off recently and reading the pages in stunned awe. I couldn't believe some of the quotes and insights that I had written; they were so profound. They didn't even sound like anything I would have penned personally, yet it was my handwriting. When I put a chronology on the time I wrote in those journals, it was in close proximity to the death of my parents and also when April and I were going through some marital valleys. All the words I had written had been scribbled in the depths of suffering and loss!

COUNSELORS LOVE JOURNALS

Whatever you do, don't waste this opportunity to hurry to your favorite office supply store and get a journal that can be your companion over the next few months. I usually assign my counselees the task of journaling through some of their experiences in an effort to gather good data. This is especially effective with men because of their propensity for coming to the office and forgetting everything that happened that week. If I can get good data in the form of a daily guided journal, I can usually get helpful information.

JOURNAL MORE, TALK LESS

One of the biggest fears we have from being around hurting people is their propensity for finding a way to share their stories. Don't even act like you don't know who I am talking about: those people who take a hollow "how are you" from someone as an invitation to spill every insignificant detail about their marriage crisis. Maybe you are this person. If you are, I have a message for you. Stop!

A way to avoid becoming this person is to use a journal to write down feelings, details, and ideas. The use of a journal may diffuse your desire to bend every set of ears you see. It will give you an outlet to express your feelings in a way that will be useful later on. Keep your confidants down to one or two godly people, and have a respectful way to tell other friends fewer details.

DOCUMENT BECAUSE YOU WILL FORGET

Having spent a great deal of time in courtrooms, I sincerely hope that you will never have to be in such a place, but just in case your situation leads to that, you must be prepared. It is important to include details such as places, dates, and times for the sole purpose of protecting yourself. If your spouse pursues matters legally, you need to have all the information possible to be prudent and accurate. Something as simple as a chronological journal or diary carries a great amount of weight in a courtroom. It may also become a useful tool if both you and your spouse end up in marriage counseling. Your spouse will be less prone to deny a well-kept journal. I am not saying it's fool-proof, but it's just a good practice to keep good notes.

PLAY BY PLAY IS NOT NECESSARY!

A common trait among those in marital crisis is to feel the need to report hourly—if not minutely—on everything they are experiencing. They have a group of contacts on speed-dial that they begin to call when the urge arises, and such behavior leads to the point that even the closest friend begins to dread the call. It's not that the friend doesn't care, but let's be honest. Nothing ever gets resolved by those phone calls. The calls never seem to be about resolution. They are nothing but re-hashing and dwelling, none of which is biblical or helpful. The counselee who exercises such habits is not looking for help from Christ, but from a person. If I were to track all of my counseling experiences, I would find most of this type of counselee in the same shape as they were before seeking counseling. I would find that nothing had changed in their situations. They made no noteworthy changes and are still fixated on venting to friends.

I want to acknowledge the hurt and pain such a spouse may be feeling. I in no way want to minimize or belittle their pain, but I cannot condone repetitive and endless dwelling as a healthy form of healing. It will drive away the closest friends and strain close relationships. I urge you to wear out your pen rather than the ears of all your friends. It may hurt you to read this, but it is important that you gear your communication toward enduring and overcoming as opposed to dwelling and brooding. Dwelling and brooding is no better than doing what the young boy in chapter one did. Instead of treating his wounds, he ran and made treatment impossible.

DISCUSSION QUESTIONS

1. Discuss some reasons why you should document your feelings and experiences in a journal.

2. Explain why you should limit the number of people to whom you tell your story.

3. Write down some tactful ways to respond to the people who ask for details regarding your story.

4. What are some ideas you have on why you should journal?

INSIGHTS

MARRIAGE TRIAGE

God's Grace Never Leaves

Own Your Sins and Failures

Document Your Thoughts and Experiences

Counsel with Godly People

Adapt To Your Circumstances

Respond Biblically

Endure Through Your Circumstances

Shield Your Heart

The fear of the Lord is the beginning of knowledge; Fools despise wisdom and instruction.

~Proverbs 1:7

CHAPTER SIX

COUNSEL WITH GODLY PEOPLE

WHEN YOUR HEART IS BROKEN and you feel like your marriage is dying, it can be comforting to listen to a multitude of friends and family members who wish to ease your pain. In many cases some of the most practical and protective advice will come from your mom and dad. Parents had one primary duty as they raised you, and that was to protect you because they loved you. Even when you were no longer a child, they may have continued to harbor that desire to protect you. They wish for you to be safe and free from pain, and as a married adult, some of your pain may come from your hurtful and wayward spouse. I have heard numerous parents conclude that their daughter or son needs to "move on." As a parent myself, I can attest to the tendency to protect my own children from pain at almost any cost. It's human nature to want to protect your family, even after they move out and get married. It is important that you filter parental advice through the Scriptures to insure the counsel you receive from your parents is godly.

FAMILY ADVICE

The Bible tells us that the advice of senior adults is to be acknowledged, but only through the filter of Scripture.

A gray head is a crown of glory; It is found in the way of righteousness (Proverbs 16:31).

The counsel of family should be fall under the same scrutiny as that of any friends. Are they firm in their Christian walk? Have they responded sinfully to the way you have been treated? If a father sees his married daughter disrespected, he has to guard against sinful responses; he must be slow to anger when the natural tendency is to be swift to retribution.

Whoever is slow to anger is better than the mighty, and he who rules his spirit than he who takes a city (Proverbs 16:32).

Family members who harbor sin and unforgiveness in their hearts for the spouse of a relative are ill-equipped to offer advice. If they harbor iniquity or ill-will, then all of their counsel has the potential to be contaminated with passive-aggressive tones of animosity. Understanding that, we may need to seek biblical counsel from outside the family. Additionally, we need to think before we share details of our marital woes with our family. That could easily cause more confusion. I strongly urge any suffering spouse to seek Bible-based counsel. I have even been sought out by the sons and daughters of ministers for this very reason.

At the time of this writing, my daughter Savannah is four years old. If, after she grows up, she were to get married and have trouble in her marriage, I would refer her to a Christian counselor and would refrain from asking her for a detailed description of her marital woes. I love my daughter, and it would break my heart for her to emotionally suffer. It would be best for me not to outline what I would want to do to the man who hurt my baby girl. What my flesh would desire to accomplish is not God-honoring. For this reason, I would want someone a little more emotionally removed to counsel my daughter so that she could honor Christ in her decisions. It would be my duty as her parent to encourage her biblical obedience in the face of her difficulties.

For the parent who may be reading this, I am urging you to guide your son or daughter toward biblical counsel and remove yourself from the sphere of confidants. Ask God to use this experience to shape your heart according to His purpose. Let this empathy you feel for your children lead you into a deeper walk with Christ and not into a sinful mindset. Allow room for your son-in-law or daughter-in-law to reconcile with the family. That may not be possible if you get too deeply involved in the conflict or its details.

BLOOD ON MY HANDS

There is an incident I responded to as a police officer that is indelibly imprinted in my memory. It involved a person who attempted suicide with a firearm to the abdomen. I remember being the second officer on the scene at an apartment, and all the activity as people were scrambling about. The family was weeping and looking at me and my corporal for direction. My corporal quickly went to the suicide victim's chest. I pulled out my pocket CPR device to give breaths. As I bent down, I remembered that I had left my disposable gloves in my police cruiser, but there was no time to retrieve them. We both positioned ourselves over the body of the victim, and my corporal gave the first chest compression—at which time blood came out of the victim's mouth and all over my bare hands.

Although our first responder actions weren't really useful, we did it to provide the family with an adequate memory of someone trying to help during their loved one's death. As I relive the moment my hands were covered in blood, I can't help but regret that I wasn't properly equipped to give aid to the victim. I had left my gloves in my patrol car. It didn't matter that she would not have lived; I felt that I had let the victim down because I should have been ready.

When your marriage is in crisis, it is critical to run to godly counsel to avoid the possibility of being counseled by someone ill-equipped to address your circumstances. You need someone who is seasoned and prepared to guide you in a way that will honor Jesus Christ.

Preach the Word; be ready in season and out of season; reprove, rebuke, exhort with great patience and instruction (2 Timothy 4:2).

CAUTIONS ON COUNSELORS

There are safety precautions that need to be taken when choosing any counselor. First, never agree to meet with a counselor of the opposite gender alone or outside of an office setting. If you prefer a counselor of the opposite gender, always take along a friend who is the same gender as you. A ministry I initiated with the senior adults at Northside Baptist, Charlotte, is called *Ministry of Presence*. When a female wishes to counsel in my office outside of business hours, a senior adult comes and sits in the office next to my clear glass door. It allows for the counselee to feel safe and provides liability protection to me as the counselor. I recommend this to both small and large churches with a counseling ministry.

Also, just because a counselor's business card has the word *Christian* on it doesn't guarantee that you've found Bible-based counseling. It is important to check out your counselor before receiving guidance in any form. A great resource to find a Christian counselor is The Association of Biblical Counselors website. The ABC website provides information on how to screen a potential Christian counselor; they suggest asking the questions listed below. You can also research information at The American Association of Christian Counselors website, also known as AACC. Both of these associations have thousands of trained counselors who can guide couples and individuals through this painful season of life.

QUESTIONS TO ASK WHEN CHOOSING A COUNSELOR

1. Is God's Word the source of their counsel? Is the Bible seen as being one truth among many other truths, or is it the most reliable place for real help? Find a counselor who is convinced that real truth applied to real problems brings about real change. Lives are changed as the truth of God, as revealed in His Word, is applied to the toughest problems.

2. Is the counselor biblically sound? Most counseling errors stem from the fact that the counselor has views of God, change, problems, etc., which are shaped more by culture and pop psychology than by God's Word. Sound theology should shape their psychology rather than the other way around.

3. Is the counselor committed to growth and change, or is the counselor more interested in endless discussions about the problem? Many counselors are good at "diagnosing" but don't have answers for change.

What results is "Diagnostic Damnation." Seek out a counselor who is more concerned with God-honoring change than with labels.

4. Will the counselor lead me to answers found in God's Word, or tell me the answers are within me? Most of the 250 commonly used approaches to counseling assume "the answers are found within." Find a counselor who understands that the Bible teaches that we need outside counsel from God and His revealed truth. They should point people to real answers, not more self-focus.

5. Is the counselor well-trained? Find a counseling center that is well-trained in biblical counseling. They should provide in-house training in addition to the degrees the counselors have already received. Please check out the ABC network to help locate a biblical counseling center in your area.

6. Will the counselor honor my marriage? Much marriage counseling today is really divorce counseling. Counselors split couples up to work on "individual issues," and the end result is the couple growing farther apart. Find out if the counselor takes seriously the commandment to "not separate what God has joined together." Couples should be counseled together and work toward real changes that will grow the worst marriages into marriages that sing.

7. Will the counselor honor my authority as a parent? Some counselors meet alone with children and do not include parents in the process. Find out if the counselor will counsel kids with their parents present as well, because we believe it to be the best way to implement real change. Bible-based counseling equips parents to lead their children.[6]

JOHN AND RACHEL

Both John and Rachel knew that there was a need for the accountability of a biblically grounded third party. This was not an issue that they could walk through together without knowing someone was overseeing and measuring their progress with compassion and consistency. There were numerous sources listed on the Internet and even in the seldom used phonebook, but which one should they choose? John placed the responsibility of choosing a counselor on Rachel. He wasn't doing this to shirk a responsibility but felt that if Rachel was comfortable with the counselor, he would do all he could to be open and transparent, regardless of his feelings.

John knew that there were many husbands out there in the world in his shoes who had not been as concessionary, and he wanted to be different. He loved his wife and desired to be forgiven and restored. He knew there would be many sleepless nights he would feel regret and pain because of Rachel's deep hurts. He knew he would have to watch helplessly as Rachel suffered because of his own selfish and sinful actions. The loss of her safe reality, and even her hopes and dreams. All the feelings of shame that would visit and re-visit them during this season of their marriage. They both would need accountability from someone to help them rebuild and restore these areas of their life. The need for biblically centered counseling would be a vital part of the restoration process in their marriage. Someone who could help focus them to see the purpose in their pain.

DISCUSSION QUESTIONS

1. What can contaminate the counsel of our friends and relatives?

2. Discuss the amount of detail you need to give your family about your marriage conflict.

3. Name some reasons it would be necessary to give your family more details. Have you been assaulted and need to seek safety?

4. Are the answers to your problems found within you? What do you do if you run across a counselor with this philosophy?

INSIGHTS

MARRIAGE TRIAGE

God's Grace Never Leaves

Own Your Sins and Failures

Document Your Thoughts and Experiences

Counsel with Godly People

Adapt To Your Circumstances

Respond Biblically

Endure Through Your Circumstances

Shield Your Heart

Come now, you who say, "Today or tomorrow, we shall go to such and such a city, and spend a year there and engage in business and make a profit." Yet you do not know what your life will be like tomorrow. You are just a vapor that appears for a little while and then vanishes away.

~James 4:13-14

CHAPTER SEVEN
ADAPT TO YOUR CIRCUMSTANCES

Are you one of those people who crumble at any sign of change and redirection? When I was an IT manager, I worked around a variety of personalities and backgrounds. I truly feel that I worked among some of the most intelligent people in their respective fields. A few of these people possessed some traits that made them the first to be picked on difficult projects, but it wasn't primarily because of their intelligence. They had been chosen because of their ability to adapt to difficult situations. I never worried about them calling me in a panic because they didn't have the proper resources or manpower. They just seemed to always have an innate ability to adapt and make it through the problematic circumstances.

MAKING PLANS FOR GOD

I left police work in July of 1997 with the intent of never going near another domestic situation as long as I lived. Ironic, isn't it? Had I followed through, I might have ended up writing something called *A Book about Anything but Marriage Conflict* rather than *Marriage Triage*. Yes, God evidently overlooked my declaration because He led me to a field of work where I'm neck-deep in the throes of marital conflict and mayhem. Isn't God hilarious? I'm just thankful that God called me out of my own selfish desire for what I considered to be happiness. He showed me through my own obstinance how His way is best. Now that I am permanently embedded in the river of marital strife—as a counselor—I understand what God was orchestrating. He has burdened my heart for those in emotional pain and agony. I desire to bring the hope of Christ to hurting spouses so that they can survive their emotional crisis.

NAKED MAN WITH A SHOTGUN

I didn't see it at the time, but God was using police work to train me to adapt to uncertainty. No scenario I entered had a program schedule, and it was a sure bet that things would not go as I planned. It meant that I had to think on my feet—and sometimes run with them. I had to be ready to react to unexpected events and remain calm and prepared. These traits could not be accomplished without being conditioned from being placed in difficult situations.

It was a busy night for police radio calls in Greensboro. I was working second shift when I received a call to respond to a domestic disturbance on Elam Avenue near the campus of UNCG. A woman had called 9-1-1, screaming that her husband was drunk and tearing up the house. I arrived on the scene first, followed by my assist car driven by a more seasoned officer. My assist officer allowed me to handle the initial contact with the hysterical woman, who was holding the hand of her young daughter. The woman didn't wait for me to walk to her door, but ran through the yard to meet me on the sidewalk.

She told me that her husband was drunk, angry, and naked. Furthermore, he was walking through the house breaking things. I told the woman that he could break his own property, and there was nothing I could do. She didn't seem satisfied with my answer. I asked her if she had been threatened or struck by her husband, but she would not give me an answer. In frustration, I told her I was leaving, and I headed toward my police car.

As I turned, I caught a surreal glimpse of something out of the corner of my eye. It was the naked husband walking onto the porch, but his nudity wasn't what alarmed me. It was the double-barreled shotgun that he was pointing directly at me!

I made a decision long before this moment about how I would handle this type of scenario. If a bad guy had the drop on me and my gun was still holstered, the only target he would be given was my big behind!

I tried to take off as hard and fast as my legs could carry me, but I wasn't going anywhere! What was wrong with me? It was like those dreams you have where you try to run and can't.

My adrenaline was so elevated that I felt as though I had lost partial hearing—which is why I couldn't hear the woman, who had latched onto my left leg and screamed at me at the top of her lungs, "Please don't shoot my husband!" I kicked the lady off of my leg, making her tumble through the yard. I had lost sight of my assist car and continued running as fast as I could to the side of the lady's house. To this day, I credit God for keeping that naked husband from pulling the trigger of that shotgun.

We cannot plan what will happen in your marriage crisis, but we must be prepared to adapt to almost any scenario we may encounter. When our spouse lets us down or threatens to leave, we must adapt in a way that honors Christ, even when it hurts. We can't give up just because we're overwhelmed and in pain. We must condition ourselves to function through it. Even if things have deteriorated to the point of separation and infidelity, you must adapt in order to avoid the temptation of letting your emotions rule your decisions. The world will tell us to strike back and get revenge, but this is not how we are instructed to respond.

WILLING TO MAKE CHANGES

Part of being adaptable involves the willingness to make changes with the goal of honoring Christ. In this modern world, people are quick to hide under the excuse that "this is just who I am." Years ago I pondered this topic from the perspective of what can truly kill a marriage.

THE MARRIAGE KILLING PHRASE

If you are hiding behind the slogan, "This is just who I am," then you have become unusable to God.

There are an endless number of marriage-killing phrases in the English language, but this one in particular can send a frigid signal to a spouse when used. You may think of phrases such as "I hate you" or "I never loved you." I could go on with a number of phrases and sayings, but I am sure anyone reading this could easily top my list with some real winners that are more potent and destructive than mine. Whatever the preferred mean and ugly phrase may be, it holds no candle to this one. It is a phrase that can even be uttered in the most harmless of ways, but it is no less venomous in its oral delivery. When the marriage-killing phrase is used, it is a declaration of selfishness that will bring an end to intimacy and growth in all areas of your marital relationship. The marriage-killing phrase is more than a feeling or emotion; it's a conscious decision one makes about his or her spouse and their relationship. The phrase I am speaking of communicates to a spouse that he or she is not worth the intentional effort to make changes in any way, shape, or form. It can even indicate that hardness has grown in one's heart in the way one wishes to present oneself or act toward one's spouse. It could mean that the one using that phrase is no longer going to fight the sinful temptations that have been struggled against for a lifetime.

Do you remember the way you presented yourself when you first met that special someone? If you are a woman, then I imagine you always tried to make sure your makeup was as close to perfect as possible. You probably watched what you said and also carefully chose your words and actions so that your potential spouse would get the best impression of you. You presented the image you wanted that special someone to see, and maybe you even changed a few of your own opinions or attitudes because you wanted to continue to present an attractive appearance and ideal behavior. You may not have even minded making these changes in yourself because you had a genuine desire to be pleasing in the eye of this potential husband. It's not that you were trying to deceive the man of your affection, but you had a genuine desire to be what he wanted in a wife. Making changes was not drudgery but a willful sacrifice for the purpose of growing closer and more intimate in the relationship.

If you are the man, chances are that you remember the way you used to present yourself to your prospective wife. You thought of small ways to get her attention. Every time she entered the room, maybe you sucked in your stomach and stuck your chest out as far as it would go! Maybe you always spoke about how you just got back from the gym where there wasn't enough weight for you to bench press—a condition I like to call *"macho-man embellishment syndrome."* If you really liked this potential bride, maybe you listened very closely to what she said so that you could learn her likes and dislikes. You needed to know if she liked yellow roses better than red roses. Maybe you listened even though listening wasn't your best quality; you simply had a strong desire to learn what pleased this woman. Perhaps you sat through some chick flicks, fighting the nausea frame by frame just to be close to that wonderful woman.

If you had some bad traits, you probably made it a point to hide these negative qualities from her. If you had a bad temper, you probably tried to keep it under control so that she would not see you in an angered condition. In fact, you may have made temporary changes in the way you normally acted to avoid revealing too much about yourself. In other words, you made some overt and willful sacrifices by turning away from your bad nature just to be close and intimate with this woman who captured your interest.

On a more personal note, I can recall many vivid memories of my wife April and I from 1992-1993, when we were dating and enjoying the time we spent together. I specifically remember the first few months of our dating life; we would sit together on the couch and hold each other and gaze in wonder. I remember the first movie we ever watched (*City Slickers*) and how we laughed and talked about so many little things. She loved my uniform and the big cop image, and I was determined to uphold the view she had of me. I tried to make small changes if I saw she liked a particular quality or behavior because I desired to have this beautiful, intelligent woman's affection.

Chapter Seven: Adapt To Your Circumstances

I had to refrain from showing my anger, critical spirit, and impatience in order to get closer to April; otherwise, she may not have wanted to be closer to me. I declared war on my carnal nature to draw closer to her and bring her into my life. In other words, I made willful and sincere sacrifices in my personality because of my love for her. What April and I didn't realize at this period of our relationship was that changing for a person never lasts, and to set a person up on a pedestal is a move destined for failure.

I am curious if anyone has been able to figure out the marriage-killing phrase from all these illustrations of personal changes we make at the beginning of a romantic relationship. If you haven't figured it out yet, then I ask that you stick with me just a little while longer while we progress through our marriage relationship. When we make changes for our spouse or fiancé, even with the best of intentions, we will begin to run into a number of detours and roadblocks. When we change ourselves for our spouse, we fail to consider that there will come a time when we will be angry, upset, and disappointed by that spouse. At times, we may not feel like behaving appropriately and graciously for emotionally motivated reasons. As the pressure begins to build, we may even tire of trying to be different. This is when the marriage-killing phrase may begin to surface in your marriage. The phrase that says, "You will just have to accept me for who I am! I don't have to change for you! You better just love me for who I am because this is as good as it gets!"

This marriage-killing phrase was seeded, planted, and watered at the commencement of the dating relationship. A man and woman came together with the idea that they would be able to change based on each other's preferences. They placed their motivation to change in a relationship with another human being who would eventually fail them either intentionally or unintentionally. We are human beings prone to sin, apart from Christ working in our lives (Romans 3:23; 1 John 4:4).

Inevitably, we all will sin and fail numerous times throughout our lives. We wake up each morning having to learn love and forgiveness all over again, many times because of the hurt we have inflicted on our spouses. The truth is that we are incapable of being motivated to change based on a single person in our lives. Even authors such as Stanton Peele fall short in this area by saying our motivation to change can rest on our spouse or children! Even Mahatma Gandhi fell short when he said, "We must become the change we want to see." The Bible tells us that if we try to change ourselves, we will not only have a relapse but will also be much worse than we were before the change (Matthew 12:43-45). This is repeatedly lived out in marriages where one spouse reverts back to his or her old ways months or years later, giving up on being the person the other spouse thought they had married!

Even though I just told you that changing for yourself or others will fail, I offer you hope. We can get past the marriage-killing phrase by understanding that only through Jesus Christ working in our lives can real transformation occur. Paul said, "But let the Lord Jesus Christ take control of you, and don't think of ways to indulge your evil desires" (Romans 13:14). Putting Christ in charge of your change will mean that he is the motivation for everything you will ever do! We make changes in our marriage because of Christ's example to us. He loved and cared for us when we were refusing to change ourselves (Romans 5:8). Furthermore, through Jesus we can become what He alone desires us to be—a new person through His transforming work in our lives (2 Corinthians 5:17). You don't have to be just who you are or who your spouse wants. You can be who Christ wants you to be, and there's nothing better!

Are you the one who has decided to settle for the relationship and situation you and your spouse currently have? Have you concluded that it's not worth the headache to make an effort to change? Maybe you have wasted countless hours trying to change for your spouse and have finally given up. Don't you see that there is hope for you after all in both your relationship to Christ and your marriage? You have wasted countless hours trying to change under your own strength and for the wrong person! Focus on your relationship to Christ first, and let him perform a transformation in your life (Philippians 4:13; 2 Corinthians 5:17). If you commit your attention to the standard Christ has set for you, then you will supersede any expectation your spouse may set for you! It means living each day of your marriage intentionally and always looking for ways to be more Christ-like in all you do each day.

The choice you have to make now is whether or not to commit your makeover to Christ and allow him to turn you into what matters more than a spouse's matrimonial checklist! You must understand that there is someone out there who loves and desires to see you become all that you can be, and His name is Jesus.

DISCUSSION QUESTIONS

1. What are some things that you can now see in your time of suffering that you didn't notice before?

2. What are some areas of your life that need to change in order for you to honor Christ?

3. What are your weaknesses in the area of adapting to change?

4. Make a list of the areas where you need to adapt and make changes. Spend some time praying over these issues.

INSIGHTS

MARRIAGE TRIAGE

God's Grace Never Leaves

Own Your Sins and Failures

Document Your Thoughts and Experiences

Counsel with Godly People

Adapt To Your Circumstances

Respond Biblically

Endure Through Your Circumstances

Shield Your Heart

If I regard wickedness in my heart, The Lord will not hear.

~Psalm 66:18

CHAPTER EIGHT
RESPOND BIBLICALLY

Right this moment, your despairing heart aches. The events that have taken place in your home have caused such a virtual earthquake that you have lost the compass of what healthy or normal is supposed to be. So much pain has entered your heart that you may not want to wait on God. I know that keying your spouse's car can seem a whole lot more satisfying than offering mercy and forgiveness. I have taken both husbands and wives to jail because of actions done in rage. Others respond to the marital earthquake with feelings of worthlessness and emptiness. Wherever you may be at this moment, I need you to understand that through Christ alone there is still purpose and hope in your life. Right now you don't see how any good could ever come of this turmoil. You aren't the first person to feel that a situation is hopeless.

Many prophets in the Old Testament watched evil pervade Israel and wreak havoc on their lives. Questions filled their minds. Why were such bad things allowed to happen to them? There was a man named Habakkuk who had the same questions as you! That's right! This minor prophet petitioned the Lord out of his frustration. He saw the enemies of God prospering over Israel. Habakkuk said,

"Why dost thou make me see iniquity, and cause me to look on wickedness? Yes, destruction and violence are before me; Strife exists and contention arises" (Habakkuk 1:3). Habakkuk literally camped out waiting for an answer from God about the progression of evil against his people. It made absolutely no sense why bad things were happening to good people!

It seems that Habakkuk is stressing the intensity and the certainty of the violence, struggles, and strife in our lives. In fact, part of his petition to God was that he wanted help making sense of it all. Habakkuk is giving a guarantee of such times in the life of Judah. It seems that God sometimes has to knock every single distraction out of the way for us to focus on the source of all our provision and security.

Habakkuk concludes by saying that he will rejoice in the Lord the God of his salvation (Habakkuk 1:18). Habakkuk began to see that God had allowed such calamity to fall upon the Israelites so that they would focus on what should be important in their lives. Maybe God is teaching you a valuable lesson that you will one day reflect upon with greater understanding. I am not in the least bit implying that God *caused* your marriage trauma, but I am saying that God uses all events such as your grief to His glory. God desires for us to prosper and have hope, but many times it comes at a great cost.

THE WRONG RESPONSE TO CIRCUMSTANCES

Clara Harris of Houston, Texas, received a twenty-year sentence in February 2003 for killing her husband, David, a Clear Lake orthodontist. Clara grabbed headlines for the circumstances behind the murder and her motive for the crime. Clara's husband had confessed to cheating on her with his receptionist but vowed to end the affair and reconcile with Clara. Clara had made many changes to win her husband back, including getting a makeover and consulting a plastic surgeon.

Prosecutors painted a picture of Harris as outraged after finding her husband with his mistress, Gail Bridges, at the Nassau Bay Hilton hotel. Not trusting him to break off his relationship with Bridges, Clara had hired a private investigator to follow him.[7] She was convicted six months after the murder, on what would have been her tenth wedding anniversary.

This may be an extreme illustration of the wrong response, but many spouses choose to address the betrayal without ever considering what Christ requires of them. They choose the destructive response that may seem satisfying at the moment, but ultimately it brings further destruction into their own lives.

There is a way that seems right to a man, but its end is the way of death (Proverbs 14:12).

A SUICIDAL RESPONSE

Dan was the center of attention wherever he went. He had such an amazing sense of humor that kept his friends in stitches. He had entertained the idea of going into police work and finally went to Basic Law Enforcement Training (BLET), receiving the certification he needed to become a sworn officer. He became an officer for a small town and soon noticed an alluring fringe benefit of his job. Women loved his uniform. He dated on a regular basis, until meeting a woman who took his breath away. Dan and the woman quickly entered into an intimate relationship, even though Dan knew it was sinful. Dan began to live with the woman several days out of the week, and he believed that the relationship was strong. Then Dan began to suspect that his girlfriend was unfaithful, and one fateful day he discovered the truth. He was so steeped in his sin at this point that it didn't even occur to him to handle his situation biblically. One night he took his service revolver, went to the foot of his bed, and took his life. He responded to his sinful circumstances with more sin.

Dan is an illustration of several friends that I knew personally who chose to respond in sinful permanence to the suffering in their life. As I write this, I can't help but reflect on a friend of mine in Greensboro who ended his life due to a custody battle with his wife. Both men rationalized that the best way to end their pain and suffering was to end their lives.

It is common for those attempting suicide to do so in an attempt to *control* their relationship with their spouse[1]. Some may ask how a person can spiral to such a low point. All it takes is for us to become obsessed with our own concerns and happiness. Once we reach this sinful mindset, it becomes easy to justify any actions or reactions. The Bible says that once we arrive at this frame of mind, we choose to *surrender* all control of our decisions to our sin. How ironic.

Therefore do not let sin reign in your mortal body that you should obey its lust (Romans 6:12).

I appeal to anyone who is thinking the world is better off without you, to seek counsel before it's too late! God has placed lasting value in your life through his son Jesus! It's easy to reason away your desire to live, but Christ loves you and wants you to endure through your crisis!

BIBLICAL RESPONSE TO EMOTIONAL MARITAL CIRCUMSTANCES

May our faith never be hinged on the expectation that God will give us what we demand, but that He will sustain us through good and bad times while displaying glimpses of His glory and power. I know this may sound rather lofty and disconnected to you right now, but it doesn't make it any less true. If you are a believer, then the Holy Spirit doesn't leave every time hurt comes into your life. The Bible teaches that Jesus will never leave or forsake us, regardless of our situation. Even if our spouses cheat and defile the marriage bed, we will never be forsaken by the One who loved us enough to die for us.

Let marriage be held in honor among all, and let the marriage bed be undefiled; for fornicators and adulterers God will judge (Hebrews 13:4).

My keen insight into the obvious has picked up on something about the nature of the God who created each of us. He is a very jealous and possessive God who desires all—not just a little—of our love and affection (Exodus 20:5). Our lack of loyalty deeply wounds God. If you are the offended spouse, then just maybe you can begin to understand just how hurt God is by our waywardness and faithlessness. Through your hurt, Christ has exposed you to a very small taste of His disappointment and pain in our actions. No sad country song ever written could adequately describe the grief we have caused Jesus. Yet, the same God to whom we have been unfaithful and wayward provided a promise for all those who believe in Him!

Let your character be free from the love of money, being content with what you have; for He Himself has said, "I will never desert you, nor will I ever forsake you (Hebrews 13:5).

Do you realize the promise that Jesus has given to His followers? Even when we fail Him, He will never leave us! Think about the ways you disappoint Him and defile your covenant with Him, and yet He is not going to reject you. I am praying that you will have an open heart toward the possibility of restoration in your marriage, but regardless of the outcome, Jesus won't leave. This also gives you the freedom to pursue restoration with the safety of having nothing to lose in Christ. I am not discounting your emotional turmoil. I am just saying that as you walk through this dark period, stay away from hopeless resolutions and phrases such as "I will never." Just be open to whatever the Bible requires of you.

Christ's presence is always there to guide and direct, but suffering can sidetrack our reception. If we get too caught up in our hurt and fail to listen to the Holy Spirit, we can make some pretty poor and reckless choices.

I sincerely believe that there is no situation we experience without God's purpose and plan in the background. Even the most intense, emotional situations can equip us for a future work that God has prepared. Experience has taught me that truth.

There was a time I suffered what I considered to be one of the most embarrassing, heart-wrenching, and disappointing moments of my life. I was at a place in the experience where I could either be challenged or become immobilized by emotions and pain. I chose to be challenged, but as I walked away, I began to reflect on current and past situations of counseling spouses in crisis. I compared them to my feelings at the moment. Although I am certain my emotions were not as intense, my feelings of disappointment, regret, and hurt helped me to see others' circumstances in a different light.

Through my own hurt and disappointment, God had created an amazing temporary filter to help me understand and better discern the hurts of those who crossed my path! The prime example of the One who experienced all our hurt, disappointment, and anxiety is Jesus.

For we do not have a High Priest who cannot sympathize with our weaknesses, but one who has been tempted in all things as we are yet without sin (Hebrews 4:15).

We know that Jesus got it right every time and remained sinless, and while we are far from sinless, we too can choose to use our times of heightened emotions to see the hand of God and the hurts of others. It sure beats poor-me pity parties where you can cry if you want to. How futile and empty! Jesus can bring purpose and comfort to our most painful life experiences.

Where are you right now? Are you in the midst of hurt, disappointment, anger, or maybe even regret? It would be so easy to just succumb to bitterness or anger, but think it through. As a Christian, what should your response be? I am not here to simply throw out a hollow cliché such as "If God shuts a door, He opens a window." That's easy to say when you are standing on the outside looking in on someone's situation, but I want to challenge you to see your situation differently. See it like Jesus sees it. Use the moments of hurt and disappointment to ask God what He wants you to see. Start using these moments to see and sympathize with the hurts of others more vividly and clearly!

RESPONDING WITH REPENTANCE

A vital aspect of responding to our marriage crisis is working to get the clutter and sin out of our lives. Even when our spouse has betrayed us, it looks ten times worse when we're harboring pockets of sin in our own lives. Failing to address our own sin can have a cascading effect that impacts our family.

THE CASCADING EFFECT OF SIN IN MARRIAGE

Sometimes people take the liberty of compartmentalizing their choices or decisions and assume those choices won't impact their spouses, children, or both. Let me ask you something. Do you believe that in the scope of your marriage that you can sin in a way that does not affect your family? Is there such a thing as a victimless sin? After all, the purpose of the vice squad is to investigate crimes that have no victim, so there must be such a thing as a victimless sin, right?

Wrong.

Maybe we need a clear definition of what sin really is before we proceed. While my policy is to avoid using five-dollar words, this time I'm going to make an exception. Sin is a "vitiated state of human nature in which the self is estranged from God" (Collegiate Dictionary). In other words, sin by its own definition propels us away from God. *Vitiated* means that you have been rendered totally ineffective when it comes to God's purpose for your life! With that in mind, look at Psalm 90:8. "You have set our iniquities before you, our secret sins in the light of your presence." Not only does our sin affect all we will ever have the privilege to experience, it is also visible—not hidden. This is why sin ought to be so putrid to our spiritual noses that it makes us physically sick. Sin holds the power to completely separate us from God if we allow it to manipulate and influence our daily lives (Romans 6:23).

I want to remind you that God has provided a way for us to be forgiven of our sins throughout the New Testament (Romans 5:8; Romans 10:9), but this does not change the fact that our sin bears consequences. It's like when our children disobey. They may say they are sorry for the wrong that they've done and receive our forgiveness, but they still receive a punishment to deter them from further disobedience.

Now we go back to my initial question of whether the consequences of our sin will affect more individuals than just the spouse who commits the sin. To demonstrate how sin's consequences reach beyond us, I would like to take you back to the 1990s when I was a patrol officer in Greensboro, North Carolina. It was around nine o'clock that night when a family was returning home from dinner on the north side of town. The daughter was driving the car, and her mother was sitting in the front passenger seat. The daughter went to make a left turn across oncoming traffic and did not give enough room to an oncoming car. That car T-boned the door on the passenger side of the vehicle. It was my duty that night to investigate the death of that mother who had been killed almost instantly from the impact of the crash. The daughter was grief-stricken and heartbroken over the loss of her mother. She was so sorry for the mistake that she had made, but nothing she did would take away the consequence of that mistake. The daughter will live the rest of her life knowing she caused the premature death of her mother. It was never the daughter's intention to inflict the slightest of injuries on her mother, but it doesn't make the outcome any less tragic.

This illustration is a perfect example of how our sinful actions can cause consequences we never imagined or anticipated. We see illustrations of how whole families were lost based on the actions of the spouse. If you're not convinced, take some time to read about David and Bathsheba. David physically and spiritually lost one child after the other because of his sin (2 Samuel 12). Take some time and read how, due to Achan's selfish sinfulness, death came to his family as well as to several more innocent men (Joshua 7:1-15).

I have a question for any Christian spouse caught up in their own sin right now. I have gone over some pretty extreme illustrations, but I want to ask a different question regarding your children or spouse. You may never cause the physical death of a child or your spouse because of your sin, but there is something that is even more final. Are you willing to stay in a state of disobedience to God at the risk of your son, daughter, or spouse suffering a spiritual death? Is the pleasure of your sin really worth risking it all?

I wish we could call heaven and speak with David about his favorite son, Absalom, and ask David how he lived with the regret of knowing he played a part in his son's rebellion and spiritual death. I believe it hurt him more than the physical death of Absalom. David's sinful and disobedient actions drove him to lust, adultery, and ultimately the murder of Uriah (2 Samuel 11). Although God forgave David for his sins, the consequences were left to be paid. And they were tragic.

One of the most reliable statistics on adultery comes from the National Opinion Research Center at the University of Chicago. In 1992 the center sent hundreds of interviewers to gather data on the sexual conduct of Americans in the National Health and Social Life Survey. In a face-to-face survey of 3,432 adults born from 1933 to 1974, researchers asked: "Have you ever had sex with someone other than your husband or wife while you were married?" A quarter of the married men in the United States and a sixth of the married women reported having at least one extramarital affair.

Some spouses have become so hurt and disillusioned that they have lost their ability to care about their sin. The irony of this scenario is that almost 90 percent of men and 94 percent of women surveyed said they believed that extramarital sex was "always wrong" or "almost always wrong."

Wherever you may be, let me encourage you to let it stop right here and now (Ephesians 4:22). God's Word can bring you out of the pit that you are in and into an obedient and content relationship with Christ (2 Peter 1:4-8). Stop listening to the voices of friendly opinion and understand that God's plan for your life has most likely been on your nightstand or book shelf all along (2 Timothy 3:16). Seek godly counsel and know that God is waiting to forgive you and to give you a second chance right now. Obediently accept his offer of forgiveness and restoration while there is still time and before the consequences grow (Romans 5:8; Romans 6:23; Romans 10:9).

A SPLITTING HEADACHE

I recall a particular third shift night in Greensboro on the northeast side of town. I was patrolling the Willow Road area just off of East Lee Street, and I remember being very sleepy and fatigued. It was probably about two in the morning, and I was so tired that it appeared that the street signs were walking. I remember looking in the distance this particular evening, and I noticed a silhouette of a person walking down the middle of the road, waving their arms like an aircraft carrier specialist. I also saw something protruding from the side of the head of this person but just assumed it to be a large pick or comb. As I closed the distance, the silhouette turned out to be a middle-aged, intoxicated female. I got my first clear look at what was in her head, and I could not believe my eyes. What I saw was surely a medical impossibility! In the side of her head, there appeared to be the wooden handle of a very large kitchen knife! The woman approached the window of my police car with a very simple and honest request. With stale beer breath and a raspy voice, she asked, "Officer, could you please get this knife out my head?" I was so caught off guard that she had to ask me twice.

I picked up my radio microphone and had an ambulance respond to my location to give the woman assistance. The emergency medical technicians transported her to the hospital, and I watched in amazement as the doctors literally beat the knife out of the woman's head with a make-shift rubber mallet. Remarkably, the woman survived with no brain damage and minimal blood loss. My investigation uncovered that the woman was stabbed in the head by her inebriated boyfriend.

The woman never once lost consciousness, though she was in a great deal of pain when the alcohol wore off. The doctors said that she could have lived like this for days without any real, ill effects, although infection would have eventually set in. Fortunately, she saw a need to seek assistance in order to have the knife removed from her head. As crazy as this may seem, there are many Christians in a similar predicament spiritually.

Sin may have cut into your life, and you go about your days without a nagging need to remove it from your spiritual anatomy. The sin may not be disturbing your daily routines yet, but there will come a time when it will spiritually injure you. The knife in your head may be bitterness, unforgiveness, and anger. You may have reached a stage where you choose to harbor hatred and animosity, which will hurt no one but you. Seek out the Christian influences that can help you remove the nagging sin from your life while there is still hope. Seek obedience to Christ by removing those sins that are impeding your relationship with Jesus.

Therefore, since we have so great a cloud of witnesses surrounding us, let us lay aside every encumbrance, and the sin which so easily entangles us, and let us run with endurance the race that is set before us (Hebrews 12:1).

A WORD JUST FOR HUSBANDS

Part of responding biblically is to acknowledge what you were doing wrong to begin with. In my marriage, I came to a place where I had to assess if I was guilty of not nurturing and cherishing my wife. Over a period of time, I came to realize that I had failed miserably in this area of my husbandly duties.

A key action for husbands is to respond biblically by showing the wife that she is valued. Many husbands may utter the words, but few show it in their behavior. A question to dwell upon is if we truly value our wives.

DO YOU VALUE YOUR WIFE?

We will know, study, and spend time with what we value.

According to Encarta, *value* is the worth, importance, or usefulness of something to somebody. To a scuba diver, an oxygen tank may hold irreplaceable value. If you are a programmer, then a computer may hold great value to your efforts. And a husband? A biblically obedient husband understands that apart from his relationship with Christ, his wife is the most valuable treasure in his life (Ephesians 5:25)!

While working for a large company, I once had the privilege of dining with one of my vendors so we could discuss some important business and negotiate some matters pertaining to our companies.

Somehow the conversation shifted from work to spiritual matters, and we began to discuss the vendor's marriage. The conversation went into deep waters rather quickly as we began to discuss things about the vendor's wife, family, and his hobbies. It turns out that the vendor was an avid golfer who enjoyed spending many hours away from home with his golf buddies at an average of eighty dollars a round. I asked him how long he had been married, and he told me only two years with no kids.

Something seemed to change in his countenance when we went from golf to marriage. I pried a little deeper and asked him what his wife enjoyed doing. The vendor said his wife was a school teacher who was immersed in her job in Charlotte. He could not name one single thing his wife enjoyed doing in the form of an activity or hobby. I also noticed the perplexed expression on his face as I dug into this area of his life that appeared to be lacking.

Over the course of twenty minutes, I learned that after two years of marriage, his wife was anything but a priority and that the influence of his in-laws and his own hobbies were creating mounting friction in the relationship. Not being able to let it go, I asked one more question. "Do you see any issues with your scenario?" The expression I received was priceless and sad all rolled into one. There are some additional complexities in this relationship that I will not go into, but there is a high probability that this relationship is headed the wrong way. I can picture the husband staring surreally at an empty bed one day, asking himself, "What went wrong?"

Again, we will know, study, and spend time with what we value. The husband in this situation read, studied, and immersed himself in the game of golf. He took lessons on improving his swing, invested in expensive clubs, and spent thousands of dollars on green fees so he could improve his game. He understood that his hobby took precision, practice, and finesse. What returns will the husband receive from all this effort? Will it move his wife to draw closer to him? Will the wife be instilled with a sense of her purpose and value to this husband? I could pile on here, but ultimately the only thing the husband will gain is a selfish sense of satisfaction and accomplishment that will hold no value when he leaves the parking lot of the golf course. Don't get me wrong; I'm not telling anyone to boycott golf. This illustration could apply to any hobby. Ultimately, anything that a husband values more than his wife will have no appreciable return. A husband cannot honor God if he values stuff more than his wife.

Husband, I encourage you this week to spend time listening to, studying and learning what your wife desires, wants, and enjoys. Understand that it is a lifetime pursuit that requires continuous study, adjustment, and practice. Love isn't something we fall into like an open manhole; it's something we learn new and fresh every day! It's not something we simply try out and throw away, but an action we demonstrate to our wives moment by moment. It can become exciting and adventurous in ways you could never begin to imagine!

I encourage husbands to give their wives more than one and two-word answers to the questions that are on their hearts. Go deep with each other and show that you value and treasure your relationship with her. Do this by sincerely opening up your heart to her and showing sincere interest in her opinions and desires.

Most of all, I want to be sure that you place your wife second while placing Christ first (Ephesians 5:25). As you have no doubt learned, hence the presence of this book in your hands, is that there will be moments in your marriage where all you have is your obedience to God to get through a difficult trial or temptation.

As we wrap up this chapter, let me direct you to a few useful Scriptures related to your marriage:

Submit to each other (Ephesians 5:22-24).

Don't live in constant conflict (Matthew 12:25).

Husbands, love your wives as Christ loved the church, because our relationships are to be a model of Christ's relationship with us (Ephesians 5:25).

God's design is for man not to be alone (Genesis 2:18-25).

Our marriages are to be intimate and fulfilling, and both husband and wife must promote and work toward that goal (Genesis 2:18, 24).

DISCUSSION QUESTIONS

1. Discuss some steps to responding biblically to your circumstances.

2. Explain the importance of prayer and Bible study in your decisions.

3. What are some unbiblical responses to issues in your marriage?

4. What is meant by responding with humility?

INSIGHTS

MARRIAGE TRIAGE

God's Grace Never Leaves

Own Your Sins and Failures

Document Your Thoughts and Experiences

Counsel with Godly People

Adapt To Your Circumstances

Respond Biblically

Endure Through Your Circumstances

Shield Your Heart

And after you have suffered for a little while, the God of all grace, who called you to His eternal glory in Christ, will Himself perfect, confirm, strengthen and establish you.
~1 Peter 5:10

CHAPTER NINE
ENDURE THROUGH YOUR CIRCUMSTANCES

I COMMEND YOU FOR YOUR curiosity and persistence on making it this far. As we near the finish, I pray that you will continue to soul search and listen to the Holy Spirit who provides comfort and direction through this process. It's likely that you or your spouse is in a spiritually weak condition right now. You may be married to a non-believer; maybe you were both non-believers at the time of your wedding. Whatever the case may be, when you spoke your vows before God and to one another, you didn't say, "For better or best, for richer or richest, in health and in perfection." Your spouse may be in a very poor spiritual condition, but you must vow to persevere and fight for your marriage, regardless of their current state of mind.

The toughest part of enduring through difficult times is that there is no guarantee of the outcome. It is easy for others to say that God will see you through, but it's another thing to actually believe and understand it. How does a person trust God without any idea what the outcome of the situation will be? When the love seems gone, it is hard to cling to any level of certainty that God will remain at your side, but somehow He always comes through.

ARMY BASIC TRAINING

I was in Army basic training in Lawton, Oklahoma, in 1983. It was quite an experience being a thousand miles from home and being constantly supervised by a grumpy drill sergeant who thought my last name was moron. You may think I'm making this up, but my drill sergeant's last name was Knuckles. He was hard-core Army. We used to go out on long hikes that would always turn into quick-time jogs and, boy, did I hate it! Many times the sergeant would let us know about how far we had to go but would then push us to run just a little bit farther. Sometimes the only thing that kept me going was the knowledge that it wouldn't last forever. I knew that at some point we would reach the end, and I could finally take a rest from my labor. Although I didn't know exactly where the finish line was located, I knew it was somewhere ahead in the distance. It's just like Peter's pep-talk letter to the persecuted Christians.

And after you have suffered for a little while, the God of all grace, who called you to His eternal glory in Christ, will Himself perfect, confirm, strengthen and establish you (1 Peter 5:10).

The hardest part of the marriage crisis is that you can never be sure what the future holds. Your spouse may turn and change, or not, and such uncertainty can be debilitating. You want to know when it will end or when to pack your things, and it seems like you are running without any hope of a finish.

WHEN CAN I MOVE ON?

A question that all suffering spouses may have pertains to when it is okay to give up and move on. All they want to do is get away from the constant source of pain and strife. They want to start over, to be close to someone who will treat them with value and care. Staying in a crisis situation seems so counter-productive to getting on with life and, depending on a person's worldview, leaving could be the right action to take. I didn't say biblical, just right from their pragmatic point of view. I have lost sleep over the topic of moving on— primarily because I cannot advise anyone to go against what the Bible clearly directs us to do.

What does *moving on* mean, anyway? To move on is to no longer give any effort to reconciling with your spouse. It may mean to forgive that spouse while at the same time conceding that neither of you are interested in pursuing marital restoration.

One reason that a relationship may have come to this crossroad is because an adulterous spouse continues to live in open sin with another partner. There is no avenue for the offended spouse to come back, because their mate refuses to allow for reconciliation. Under those terms and conditions, the offended spouse may have to withdraw, but that does not necessarily mean that they need to hurry on to a new relationship. Even if the marriage dissolves into a divorce, I would still caution a spouse to steer clear of a new relationship before working and praying through all the emotional damage and destruction.

I was born in Tuscaloosa, Alabama, and it is a place that is very special to me. On May 1, 2011, I had the opportunity to walk the streets of Tuscaloosa after the visitation of the tornado outbreak better known as April's Wrath—a tornado system that injured 2,000 people and claimed 136 lives. I witnessed communities that were literally erased from the map and people rummaging through rubble just hoping to find a token of a lifetime of memories. Even a year later, some of those communities and businesses still have not been restored to a usable state. It sometimes takes a great deal of time to renew and restore that which has been destroyed.

Can you imagine how senseless it would be to begin building on those devastated communities without first cleaning out and removing all the debris? It's the same with your own heart and emotions now. Move slowly and deliberately as you navigate through your emotional pain and devastation. Maintain your focus on healing and growing through this season of your life.

When your spouse wants to put distance between the two of you, then I encourage you to put your focus on Jesus and nurture your relationship with Him. Don't turn your attention to another person who may dilute the substance of what Christ is doing in your personal relationship with Him. You are building and strengthening your bond with Christ, and you don't need a third person to interfere with this special season. Stay focused on Christ and take preventive measures to protect yourself from any outside interference during this season. Don't place yourself in a situation to relive the same mistakes. It's not time to build again, but to heal and learn. Christ is giving you a chance to strengthen and renew your relationship with Him.

IF MY SPOUSE EVER _____, THEN I WILL NEVER!

Many spouses call adultery the trump card at the end of a relationship, but is this really irreconcilable? It seems to be the most egregious offense that a spouse could ever commit against a mate. There are even some commonly used Scriptures that a betrayed spouse can whip out and throw in their mate's face. We see sexual sin as unredeemable.

And I say to you, whoever divorces his wife, except for immorality, and marries another woman commits adultery (Matthew 19:9).

Sexual sin seems to bring spouses to their very knees, and in many compromised relationships, it is never remedied. Each spouse leaves and takes all their hurt and lack of trust into a new relationship, but they never really learn anything. Can you think of one example where an unredeemable and filthy relationship has been restored to a brand new condition? If you are a Christian, then you have one clear example of the power of redemption. Christ didn't restore you to something you were but renewed you into something that you had never been! Be careful not to write your spouse off because you don't think you can ever fully trust that person again. Use your crisis and allow something to come out of it that will mold you into a more refined child of God.

Therefore if any man be in Christ he is a new creature; the old things passed away; behold, new things have come (2 Corinthians 5:17).

Since Christ never wrote you off, I encourage you not to write off your spouse, no matter how hopeless things appear. Commit yourself to praying for your spouse, even without the guarantee of a favorable outcome. Shield your heart from other entanglements and take this time to grow more intimate with Jesus. Be an ambassador before the throne of Christ for your wayward spouse in both sickness and in health.

IN SICKNESS AND IN HEALTH

We have all heard this wording in a wedding vow before. "To have and to hold from this day forward, for better or worse, for richer or poorer, in sickness and in health, to love and to cherish from this day forward until death do us part." Most of us have said a similar if not the same vow, but did you ever really consider what it means to stay with someone through their sickness? As husband and wife, we both play an important role in the physical, emotional, and spiritual health of our spouse. When we first made these promises at the altar, it sounded like a fairly simple proposition to be there during the good and bad times, but through the years we see that there are complexities in our relationships that we never could have anticipated!

To have and to hold during sickness is more than simply running to the drug store and picking up a prescription for your spouse. Enduring through the seasons of sickness in your marriage requires a great deal of self-sacrifice and effort that rarely brings recognition. Some of the symptoms of this sickness could make a spouse want to "wash their hands" of the entire relationship. The truth is that many do.

I want us to examine three categories of sickness we will face in our marriages and recognize what the symptoms may look like. I am not a medical doctor, so don't worry about any long medical terms or phrases you may read. We will stick to laymen's terms. I am nothing more than an assistant to the master heart surgeon, administering Bible-based direction to sick hearts (Jeremiah 17:9):

The heart is more deceitful than all else and is desperately sick; Who can understand it?

PHYSICAL SICKNESS

When our spouse suffers from a physical sickness, it can manifest itself through a wide variety of symptoms. A spouse who is diagnosed with cancer may suffer from nausea, pain, and weakness throughout the body. It may require the use of chemotherapy or radiation, which could result in physical changes in the way our spouse appears. Hair or weight loss becomes a big possibility. It may affect the way your spouse treats you due to a lack of strength or energy and the inability to meet your needs. Your spouse may treat you rudely and say things that would not normally be said by a loving and healthy spouse. If a spouse has surgery or heart issues, you out of necessity may be required to carry a bigger part of the load in the day-to-day household duties. It may be burdensome for you to do more, but you understand that your spouse is sick, and you want to honor your commitment to endure in the relationship.

Of course, you don't help and assist your spouse with the motive that the favor will be returned at a later time. You do it out of love and commitment. A spouse doesn't change their beloved's bed pan or a colostomy bag because it's fun; it's done out of love and commitment to the sick spouse. An honorable spouse wants to be there for the other spouse through the sickness as well as the health part. It is an unconditional act of love and service that honors their commitment and, at the core of their Christian life, it honors God.

EMOTIONAL SICKNESS

Emotional sickness comes in a variety of conditions that can range from personality disorders to depression. Depression can drain the life out of a relationship because of the tendency to withdraw and push away from your spouse. Whether the depression is chemical, spiritual, or a combination of both, it can make a spouse feel extreme loneliness and abandonment even when they are in a crowd. Those suffering from depression do not go out of their way to meet the needs of their mates. They may even withdraw to the point of spending the majority of each day in silence. It is a hard and difficult road for those married to those who are depressed, and the only way to make it through those times is to endure with God's help.

You have to realize that your efforts to care for your spouse may not be reciprocated, but that's when your desire to obey God and honor your commitment must be enduring and resolute (2 Timothy 1:9). The endearing qualities and traits that first drew you to your spouse may have vanished, but your commitment was to honor him or her without regard for any particular emotional state. You can only pray that your spouse is going through a season of emotional sickness and will come out well somewhere along the way. It is a season that will greatly test how you define the word *unconditional*. Will you define it the way the world sees it, or will you interpret it as Christ has shown you?

Who has saved us and called us with a holy calling, not according to His own purpose and grace which was granted us in Christ Jesus from all eternity (2 Timothy 1:9).

SPIRITUAL SICKNESS

Spiritual sickness can manifest itself in an infinite number of ways, some of which may go in some rather extreme directions. The peculiar thing about spiritual sickness is that it can manifest itself in what we *don't* do as much as what we *do*. We refer to this as *sins of omission,* where we fail to be the person God desires for us to be. Spiritual sickness comes on the strongest from failing to spend time in God's Word, failing to pray, or praying with the wrong motives. It is not always easily diagnosed because the spiritually sick person may wear the mask of a spiritually healthy person. They do this by continuing to attend church and social functions as though nothing is really wrong, and they know the religious lingo.

A spiritually sick person may treat their spouse in an ungodly fashion. This person may even be tempted to succumb to sins outside the confines of marriage such as cheating. This person may fling abusive, hateful words at the spouse and use critical language. Overall, a spiritually sick spouse is in very poor condition and in need of acute care, but how do we provide that care? (Remember, we did commit to sickness and health!)

You may think I have just turned the key in the lock of an inescapable marriage prison, but let's think about this for a moment. All sin, meaning our selfishness, poor choices, words, and actions, stems from spiritual sickness (Jeremiah 17:9; Romans 3:23). When we are spiritually sick, we are incapable of making the right choices and will be more likely to choose sin and selfishness before holiness (Romans 6:12). In a marriage, that sin can be something especially repulsive and damaging. If we think about sins in marriage, we think of behaviors such as lying, abandonment, deception, substance abuse, adultery, and verbal abuse. Maybe a husband is failing to be the spiritual leader in his home and has not nurtured a Jesus-centered family. He may see the cascading effects of his own sin play out in the life of his spouse or children (1 Timothy 3:4-5). There are other sins we could list, but this gives you an idea of the categories of spiritually sick sins that can occur.

You may be anxious to discover how we go about treating the spiritually sick spouse, and I'm about to share the answer with you. I may receive a lot of excuses about why it isn't possible to help such a spouse. That's only to be expected. I understand that it's hard to play doctor to a spouse who is spiritually sick or unresponsive. That sickness may manifest itself through acts that you feel are a direct attack on you, but please understand that they aren't. Any spiritually sick spouse is sinning directly against God first. They are in a state of selfish and sinful rebellion that needs triage! Yet this is when the offended spouse is more likely to become pragmatic and "jump ship" to escape from continuing hurt.

TREATING YOUR SPIRITUALLY SICK SPOUSE

The first step in the process of treating your spiritually sick spouse is to make sure that you are not part of the problem. If you are the husband, then you need to reflect upon whether you have been the sincere spiritual leader and loving husband in your household. You will need to begin the process of change in yourself and ask God to forgive you for your failure and sin and ask Him to teach you how to be a sincere spiritual leader. The Bible says it would be better to put a huge stone around your neck and jump into deep waters than to hypocritically mislead even one little one (Luke 17:2). Instead of focusing on the spiritual sickness and sin of your spouse, first take time to focus on yourself and where you have fallen short. No surgeon's assistant walks into an operating room to perform surgery with dirty hands! The more you focus on yourself and your own obedience to God, the more useful and divinely able you will be to help your spiritually sick spouse.

You can't put a time limit on how long this may take. Becoming who God wants you to be takes endurance and lots of time. It takes more than a thirty- day boot camp to become the person God wants you to be. Be patient with yourself and God's work in your life, and you will learn to be patient with your spiritually sick spouse (Isaiah 40:31; Romans 12:12). Always remember that your spouse did not begin acting this way overnight; it is usually something that took place through years of conditioning and treatment. You can't expect everything to get better in months, and some cases, years. It may be painful to entertain such an idea, but what about the faithful wife and mother married to an unbeliever, who prays for her husband for thirty years before he becomes a believer? I hope and pray you are not experiencing this type of scenario, but you must understand the commitment you made. You must be patient. In fact, the Bible tells us that your trials will produce a great deal of patience (James 1:2-4).

The second step in the treatment process is never to give up on your spiritually sick spouse, no matter how hopeless the situation appears. You must endure and strive to support him or her through fervent prayer! Don't misunderstand what I am saying. As a former police officer, I know that there are times that your love must be given from a safe distance, in the case of abuse, but in that distance you shouldn't be quick to join an online dating service and pursue a new relationship. Ephesians commands husbands to love their wives as Christ loved and gave himself for the church (Ephesians 5:25).

When you consider how Christ was treated by the church, it puts a solemn perspective on the emotional hurt we must endure from our spouses. Let me remind you that you weren't called to happiness in your marriage, but to holiness in Christ Jesus. It doesn't feel pleasant to be verbally mistreated by the one you love and to have your kindnesses rejected, but Jesus gave us an example to follow by what he allowed Himself to be subjected to out of His love for us. Jesus never gave up on us even when we were living in open and willful rebellion against him (Romans 5:8). We were terminal in our sins, and He revived us! Here is a lesson for husbands when it comes to their wives. Stop thinking a wife is replaceable and see her for what she really is. She is a redeemed child of God, forgiven through the sacrificial blood of Jesus Christ—just like you!

The third step in the treatment process is to love your spouse no matter what the circumstances.

Love each other with genuine affection, and take delight in honoring each other (Romans 12:10).

And a woman who has an unbelieving husband, and he consents to live with her, she must not send her husband away. For the unbelieving husband is sanctified through his wife, and the unbelieving wife is sanctified through her believing husband; for otherwise your children are unclean, but now they are holy (1 Corinthians 7:13-14).

Paul wrote this to teach the church how they should love one another. If he wrote this to Christians in general, how much more does this apply to our spiritually sick spouses? We need to love them even when they push away and act as though they are repulsed by our love. I have even heard testimonies from unfaithful husbands about how much a wife's unconditional love brought them back to biblical obedience.

I took a walk with a husband one day. He was separated from his wife but still living in the same house for financial reasons. As we walked along, the husband began to vent to me that his wife had come to church but wouldn't go into a Sunday school class. I held up my hand and stopped him. I asked the husband if he had heard the words he has just said to me. I told him that what I had just heard from his lips was that because of his consistent example, his wife had come to church! Regardless of his wife's motives, the husband's wife had come to church, and that was something to celebrate!

Consider the way we treat Jesus many times in our own lives when we give in to selfishness and self-centeredness. If Christ still loves us, how much more should we endure in love toward our spouses? Don't give into that carnal feeling to declare your relationship dead, because Christ never gave up on you! Husbands, love your wives just like Jesus enduringly loves us! Listen to me good! It is never your responsibility in the relationship with your spiritually sick spouse to declare him or her dead to you! God hates divorce (Malachi 2:16). If your spouse walks away from you and breaks the covenant, then that's something you cannot prevent. Just don't be the one who is eager to end things and walk away. God may be in the process of refining you in ways you never dreamed if you just endure and guard your heart.

OBEDIENCE GIVES NO RELATIONSHIP RESTORATION GUARANTEES

The fourth and final step in this treatment process is to leave the results in God's hands and be patient (Romans 8:28). Let me answer the question you may be considering. The question is whether there is any guarantee of what the results will be, and my answer is yes. The result for those obedient spouses who choose to endure with their spiritually sick spouses is that their lives will be miraculously changed forever. You cannot control the way the spiritually sick spouse will respond to your obedience, but that should not be the primary purpose of your actions. Your primary purpose is to walk in holiness and obedience to God's direction for your life. That clear-cut direction will demonstrate unconditional and relentless love for your spiritually sick spouse, regardless of the outcome.

WE OWN OUR SINFUL SICKNESS

I want to be sure there is no confusion about spiritual sickness and my use of the phrase. Every Christian is responsible for his or her own choices and decisions. When we choose to turn toward sin, we run the risk of becoming enslaved to it. The question is: who chose to sin?

Jesus answered them, "Truly, truly, I say to you, everyone who commits sin is the slave of sin" (John 8:34).

COUNT IT ALL JOY TO SUFFER?

James is a favorite New Testament book of mine. James addressed his letter to Jewish Christians scattered outside of Palestine because of persecution and induced dispersion in most cases. These Jews must have been disillusioned and even disheartened and tired. They stood up for their faith! They were faithful to Christ at the risk of losing family ties and friends! Security through their trade was found in their home city(s) along with a sense of oneness and purpose. So why is it they had to flee from their homes out of fear of persecution and death? Wasn't following Jesus supposed to be convenient and easy? Since they were being shunned by the Jewish community, they had no way to buy or sell goods in their own city.

James was addressing the Diaspora, which refers to people who have been scattered from their homes in Jerusalem. I like how the New World Encyclopedia says it even better; it speaks of people forced or induced to leave Jerusalem because of their conversion from Judaism to Christianity. With all of that in mind, James told the Diaspora to count it all joy as they experienced such a trial!

When I ponder these truths in the framework of marriage, I can see how a spouse might feel this same sense of frustration. You have remained faithful throughout your marriage and sought to remain committed in every way. You have gone out of your way to make your spouse feel loved and adored, and yet you are now suffering through trials of infidelity or deceit in your marriage! You are experiencing the looks of those around you who don't understand. You feel judged, lifeless, and hopeless. The question is how do you rejoice in such painful circumstances? As illogical as it may seem, I am challenging you to find a way because of what the book of James tells us. You may not even be able to do it as you finish reading this paragraph, but I am urging you to pray it through and give it your most valiant effort.

What do you need to rejoice about today in the midst of your suffering? It should not be a surprise that this moment has come, because even James told us that it was a case of "when," not "if." Hang in there and rejoice. God will reveal his purpose in His time. Even if your suffering is directly related to your faith, remain hopeful that Christ will see you through.

COPING AND ENDURING THROUGH PAIN IN YOUR MARRIAGE

Some may ask what right a person has to comment on emotional hurt and loss, which is a fair question. One may say that before anyone can write about coping with pain, that person must have experienced pain to the same level. In my case, pain came from loss. I lost my sister in 1964, and although I was born in 1963, I watched the effects of that loss on my mother throughout my life. I was very close to my father, and I lost him to a heart attack in 2000. Then, I watched my mother grieve herself into poor health. In 2003 she was hospitalized with a brain aneurism, leaving me and my brother to make decisions regarding the life support that was in place. Mom died four days later as my brother and I watched her breathe her last breath here on earth. My mother's death was almost three years to the date of my father's.

Emotional pain has visited my life, and in the following story, I will briefly describe the source of my strength through an eventful bike ride. May this story encourage you wherever you may be on your emotional journey.

BICYCLING

I have developed a real passion for bicycling. I am by no means a Lance Armstrong follower, and I don't follow the Tour de France, but I love riding. I typically stay in the vicinity of North Carolina where my wife April and I can find new and interesting places to take our bicycles and spend time together. There is something that any good cyclist knows is necessary to enjoy more distant rides across a larger span of territory, and that is the need to condition oneself to ride through quite a bit of pain.

The other day I arrived home before my family and decided I would take a nine-mile trek down some new roads near our house. All was good as I hit Oakwood and went onto Rogers Lake Road. I had to be extremely careful because the road was only two lanes, and cars typically trump bicycles when it comes to getting knocked off the road.

As a car was coming up behind me, I pulled to the far right side, and my tire dropped off the shoulder of the road. It wasn't necessarily a problem at first, but I noticed the shoulder was becoming taller as I continued to roll, and then my front tire became wedged to the point where I couldn't steer the bicycle. I tried to keep the bike up, but to no avail. I was thrown sideways onto the road, and my bicycle landed on top of me. Pain shot through my left leg, my arms, and my hands. I looked down and saw a kneecap suffering from a bloody road rash. At this point, it would be safe to assume that I said "ouch." I took a moment to thank God that I wasn't run over by a car, truck, or larger-sized conveyance. Astonishingly, somehow my bike didn't appear to have a single significant scratch or dent on it.

Standing on the side of the road in a fair amount of pain, I realized that I had a bit of a problem. I was too far from home to simply walk my bicycle back, and there was another seven miles left of my journey! Could I honestly quit my mission all because of a little pain, or did I need to finish the race? I decided on the side of the road that although I wasn't looking forward to pumping my injured and bleeding kneecap up and down for another seven miles, I had to finish my mission. I remounted my bicycle and began to pedal. (Don't expect me to confess to any potential girly-man sounds I may have made over the next mile or so.) As I continued to pedal and focus on the road and attempt to enjoy the scenery surrounding me, I began to forget that I had fallen earlier in the journey. In fact, there were a few things I was now doing on my bicycle to avoid what happened earlier. That is to say I had learned from my past mistake. I was now focused so much on my mission that the pain became secondary to me, and I was honestly enjoying the ride!

What pushed me to continue when I began to feel the pain and burn was the knowledge that it wouldn't last forever and that rest and refreshment were waiting for me at the finish! As I pulled into the driveway of my home on mile nine, I felt a burst of exhilaration that came from knowing that I finished my mission and didn't quit. While I didn't break any time trial records on my trip, that had never been the purpose, anyway. It was never about how good I was but about finishing what I had started.

Many Christians believe that a life in Christ is a pain-free existence, but this has never been the case. Jesus never promised His followers that they would suffer no pain in this life. In fact, Jesus told Peter a time would come in his life when he was older when he would stretch out his arms and be placed somewhere he did not want to go. (We believe he was referring to Peter dying from crucifixion.) Peter went on to write that if any man suffers as a Christian, let him not be ashamed (1 Peter 4:16). Peter emphasizes this again in the same letter where he tells believers that their comfort comes from knowing that the suffering will have a duration of time but will not last forever (1 Peter 5:10).

Given a choice, no one would voluntarily choose a life of suffering and pain. But we live in a fallen world. Christians are not immune from painful experiences in our walk. Becoming a Christian does not involve the issuance of a halo and a hovercraft! Our lives may be tough, and sometimes the pain may seem unbearable, but there is good news. Our suffering is limited to this life, and our coming comfort and contentment will last forever. Paul tells us that we don't have to grieve as those who have no hope (1 Thessalonians 4:13). No matter what your suffering stems from, there is a comfort and peace you can constantly have that has no expiration date. You have a hope that can drive you to finish your mission through any sort of pain and suffering. Paul even said that he learned that whatever situation he was in that he could have contentment in his heart (Philippians 4:11). What state are you in today? Is it a broken marriage, grief over the loss of family, broken relationships? Are you in the "if only" mode of regret, or have you made some mistakes in your marriage that you feel will never be reconciled? I believe I could make this list quite long, but for the sake of word count I will let you fill in your own blank.

You may be at the painful point of throwing up your hands over your pain, believing that you cannot go one step further, but I encourage you today to believe that, in Christ, you can make it!

God is completing a work in you as we speak that will astound and amaze you. You may already have seen it, and in that case you know that quitting should not be an option. I exhort you to press on and find comfort in knowing that the pain won't last forever but, as Peter said, only for a little while. Let God finish the wonderful work he has begun in your life (Philippians 1:6). Finally, I ask you to do as Paul instructed: finish the race. We have not been told to win this race just as I mentioned my time was no record to brag about. We are just told to run this race without apology, pain and all! We are to run the race with persistence and patience (Hebrews 12:1). You can do it through Christ who provides the strength (Philippians 4:13).

DISCUSSION QUESTIONS

1. What kind of sickness (sin) is there in your marriage?

2. What is your biggest fear at this moment in your marriage?

3. What Scriptures sustain you with encouragement at this point in your crisis?

4. Pray that God would sustain you even when you feel like you are doing this all alone.

INSIGHTS

MARRIAGE TRIAGE

God's Grace Never Leaves

Own Your Sins and Failures

Document Your Thoughts and Experiences

Counsel with Godly People

Adapt To Your Circumstances

Respond Biblically

Endure Through Your Circumstances

Shield Your Heart

But each one is tempted when he is carried away and enticed by his own lust [desire]. Then when lust has conceived, it gives birth to sin; and when sin is accomplished, it brings forth death.

~ James 1:14-15

CHAPTER TEN
SHIELD YOUR HEART

ONE OF MY FAVORITE REQUIRED activities in police work was to go to the firing range on the north side of the city. It wasn't a nice "state of the art" indoor facility but rather a brutal, weather-enduring outdoor area equipped with nearby neighbors who loathed the sound of gunfire. We shot at man-sized silhouette targets with rings to mark the most accurate shots. Do you want to guess the location of the most valuable shot on the target? If you said the heart, you would be correct. The most vulnerable and valuable part of your anatomy is your heart, because in a critical situation, if I can attack your heart, you will not survive.

When you are in a marriage crisis situation, you are looking for a listening ear to act as though they are concerned and genuinely care. You want someone who won't judge you but will listen intently to your hurts and grievances. When this is someone of the opposite sex, it can quickly evolve into an inappropriate emotional connection. In this chapter I am going to share some scenarios that address the importance of keeping your guard up to prevent the chance of inappropriate emotional connections being formed with someone of the opposite sex. The two scenarios in this chapter offer a valuable lesson about shielding your heart from dangerous relationships when you are in the middle of a marriage crisis.

AN EXTRAMARITAL ATTRACTION

When you are intoxicated by devotion to Christ, it subdues the desire for additional inebriants.

Jennifer had known Sam for only about six months; they worked closely on a few projects together in their business unit. Sam loved playing what he considered to be harmless practical jokes on Jennifer because it made her laugh and light up. She had a beautiful smile and a magnetic personality that just made people feel at ease and comfortable around her.

Why shouldn't Jennifer seem this way? After all, she was a woman who loved the Lord heart and soul, and she was very active in her local church ministries. Her desire to be a good example for others was carried out in part by having a warm and friendly personality. She never saw any harm in letting a male coworker play jokes on her and carry on playfully each day. She never once looked at this behavior as a potential "boundary tester." She enjoyed the personal attention Sam would sometimes give her. Jennifer began to be more open with Sam about many areas of her life and even found herself sometimes staying after work to chat with him about work-related issues—and at time even more personal things.

Jennifer became so comfortable with their conversations that she didn't even begin to notice that she had been lowering her own protective boundaries that were in place to guard her heart from temptation. She rationalized away the thought that anything about her behavior with Sam might be considered inappropriate, but she began to notice that she was looking more forward to going to work each day. Jennifer even began to dress a little differently and spend more time in the morning getting ready for work. She even caught herself wearing dresses to work, which was totally out of character for her fun-loving personality. Still, she did not see anything necessarily wrong with her behavior toward Sam. They had never actually touched or even hugged each other, but emotionally she was beginning to feel something more than a casual friend should experience.

All of this playfulness and time spent in comfortable conversation would have been fine—had Jennifer not been a married woman. Has she already carried that emotional infatuation too far? Is it possible for a married woman to live out her life without ever feeling an attraction to or connection with a man who is not her husband, or is it simply a feeling we need to regulate and control?

In the scenario I have created, the husband has been very distant to Jennifer for years, and he has not been a consistent spiritual leader in his home. Jennifer has felt lonely and neglected. She has a strong desire to share an emotional connection with her husband, but he has been off his post as the guardian of Jennifer's heart for quite some time. The result is that Jennifer is now left both vulnerable and empty in her marriage, which has opened the door to outside influences. Although Jennifer is still responsible for her behavior with Sam, her husband should have never placed Jennifer in this position of temptation. If the husband fails to seek a spiritual and emotional connection with Jennifer, she could be subjected to the temptation of a man eager to give her the attention she desires. If Jennifer chooses temporary happiness instead of obedience to Christ, she will make some regretful memories she will never be able to erase.

The scenario I described above is not based on any particular couple but represents a mosaic of many couples I have dealt with over the past twenty years. Even when I was in police work, there were so many domestic incidents where husbands simply failed to fulfill their biblical roles, and in turn, the wife made some wrong and sinful choices. The result was that sin brought forth more sin. I know that some of you may not even see an issue with the friendship in this scenario because, after all, nothing scandalous happened between Sam and Jennifer, but sin doesn't start with the act, but in the heart.

Apply your heart to discipline, and your ears to words of knowledge (Proverbs 23:12).

Is it a sin to feel an attraction to someone other than your spouse? Throughout your entire life, you will sometimes feel connections, attractions, and likes for people other than your spouse for various reasons. Maybe it's a coworker, a fellow volunteer, or someone with similar outside interests to yours. Even if you have an awesome and sacred relationship with your spouse, you will still sometimes see a positive attribute in another person. This doesn't mean you must run from the presence of every human being you ever see.

The Bible has some clear direction about how to protect yourself as a spouse. Sin doesn't indulge itself at the mere temptation, but it does begin in the heart. Remarkably, it's the same path that God uses to become intimate with us. The Bible says that man looks on the outside, but God looks in our hearts. We learned this from the choosing of David to be anointed as king over Israel (1 Samuel 16:7).

Even though you may sometimes be attracted to another person, out of obedience to God and submission to your spouse, that attraction is never to be *pursued* (Ephesians 5:22-23). Even if you are married to a spouse who is not carrying their load, you are not granted the freedom to seek out someone more attractive. You are to be patient and pray daily for your spouse, asking God to change your spouse's heart. You must strengthen your own heart through prayer and Bible study (James 5:8). You are never to disrespect your spouse by being critical or derogatory in public under any circumstances (James 5:9).

In the scenario with Jennifer, we can follow the trail that led her down the road of compromise. It started out with a sense of attraction. She could have stopped there, but the positive and euphoric experience was alluring, and so she continued edging down that path. She began to feel so comfortable with Sam that she encouraged the practical joking and playfulness. She then began to spend more time with Sam and shared details of her frustration with her husband. At that moment, she demonstrated disrespect for her husband and opened up space for Sam to get emotionally closer to her. Sam knows if he just bides his time, Jennifer will eventually give in. If Jennifer does not end this behavior immediately, there is a high likelihood that she will cross more forbidden lines. The trail is quite simple to follow and is found in the book of James.

But each one is tempted when he is carried away and enticed by his own lust (Desire). Then when lust has conceived, it gives birth to sin; and when sin is accomplished, it brings forth death (James 1:14-15).

Since Jennifer dropped her guard early in the relationship when the jokes and playful behavior were occurring, she was unaware of the danger of what appeared to be harmless activity. I call this type of activity *boundary testing,* because there are times when men either knowingly or unknowingly use this type of tactic as a way to get past awkward beginnings and create a more relaxed atmosphere. In many cases it is harmless, but a married woman needs to be cautious around other men in her life. She does this out of a desire to be obedient to God, and it is also a way to show her husband respect even when he is not around.

Have you crossed any emotional lines with someone of the opposite sex who is not your spouse? Is there another person in your life right now who you constantly feel the need to defend in front of your spouse? Is it the person you think about and enjoy sharing your day with? Have you reached a point in your marriage where you just don't care anymore and just want someone who will fill the void in your life? If you take the time to nurture your relationship with Jesus Christ, then I can assure you he can give you the strength to resist those moments of temptation that may be attacking you even now. He will give you the strength to resist when the temptation is the greatest.

Submit therefore to God. Resist the devil and he will flee from you. Draw near to God and He will draw near to you. Cleanse your hands, you sinners; and purify your hearts, you double-minded (James 4:7-8).

PRACTICAL WAYS FOR HUSBANDS AND WIVES TO GUARD THEIR HEARTS

- If you are in an emotional relationship with a person of the opposite sex outside of your marriage, sever the ties immediately! (Ephesians 4:22)
- Passionately study the Scriptures, or you will compromise!
- If you work around a person of the opposite sex whom you find appealing, avoid spending time alone with that person and keep your personal life matters to yourself. If that person continues to

be a temptation, find a Christian accountability partner to help you remain pure in your marriage and to pray with you.
- Never tell a person of the opposite sex that you find him or her attractive.
- Never dine alone with a person of the opposite sex who is not your spouse or other family member.
- Always pray that God would increase your desire for your spouse in your marriage even when that spouse is living in disobedience.
- If you have a spouse who will pray with you, then do so daily. If your spouse refuses, pray alone.
- Never confide in a person of the opposite sex about personal issues.
- Never have long, friendly phone conversations or frequent texting sessions with anyone of the opposite sex who is not your spouse or otherwise related to you.

There are many more we could list, but you can see the pattern of steps necessary to guard your heart.

At the time of this book's publication, my wife April and I have been married for seventeen years, and we have learned from many experiences, both terrible and exceptional. Even though at times we struggled with the issue of extramarital attraction, our personal relationship with Christ and quiet time played a key role in our reconciliation. When I am in the Word and praying with April, I see her through the filter of God's eyes, and she is utterly breath-taking to me. After seventeen years, I still get awestruck when she walks in the room. It is almost surreal to me that this beautiful, godly woman is my wife and mother of our children! It wasn't always like this; if you were to talk with April, she would say that in the early years of marriage, misery with occasional smiles was as good as she thought it would ever get.

How wonderful it has been to see how God can transform and renew the way we perceive our spouses when we become totally dependent on our relationship with Christ first and foremost! We didn't arrive in this good marital arrangement with the snap of our fingers, and we understand that as we nurture our relationship with Christ, it provides a bond of protection in our marriage. You might wonder if we've left our days of conflict behind. To tell the truth, our marriage has never been a Utopia where we floated through days straight out of "Leave it to Beaver" episodes! I have to admit that we can still have some fusses, but the recovery period and desire to reconcile is so much more resolute and genuine. We offer the issues and struggles of our marriage as a testimony to God's grace and forgiveness. If you are struggling with extramarital attraction, we encourage you to make it a struggle! A person who isn't struggling is letting temptation have control. Struggling means you are making an intentional effort to make the right choice. Don't give up! Immerse yourself in God's Word and pray daily. You can make it through Christ!

ALWAYS KEEP YOUR GUARD UP!

What does a police officer do to keep busy at two in the morning on a weekday? In an effort to keep the thin blue line secure, I will refrain from telling you everything, but I can assure you there is always something an officer can do to avoid nodding off to sleep behind the wheel.

Chapter Ten: Shield Your Heart

It was the winter of 1989, and I had been a police officer for almost two years. I was assigned to the west side of town and had just left a coffee break near interstate 40 and West Wendover Avenue. It was a great place to work at night, and there were a variety of things to do such as work traffic and check buildings. Our primary duty was to answer our calls for police service, but this night had been rather quiet.

I was caught up on all my accident and investigative reports, and quite frankly, my eyelids were getting heavy at two in the morning. I needed something to stimulate my curiosity. I already had the window rolled down in the cold weather, and I was afraid to play the car radio any louder out of fear of not hearing my police radio. As I rode east, then west, on Wendover Avenue near the postal bulk mail center, a west-bound, dark-colored, older-model, two- door Chevy Monte Carlo with a burned out headlight caught my eye. There were two teenage-looking boys in the car, and their eyes got as big as saucers when they passed me. Something just didn't seem right about them, although the only offense I had was improper equipment for the burned out headlight. Having nothing else on my plate at the moment, I chose to investigate a little further. I turned around, got behind the Monte Carlo, and picked up my radio microphone to call in a traffic stop (10-38). I had no way of knowing what I was on the brink of encountering, all because of my curiosity.

I activated my blue lights as I called in the description and tag number to communications. It appeared we were pulling off into a small driveway directly in front of the postal bulk mail center. It was a rather odd place to stop; the driver of the Monte Carlo had no place to exit or pull away since my police car was directly behind him. The driver was literally blocked in. Maybe he was not up to anything, so there was no need for him to have an exit strategy. Whatever the driver was thinking, I could not simply assume the best. I had to keep my guard up, and for some reason I still felt very ill-at-ease about this particular traffic stop.

I stepped out of my police car and carefully surveyed the movements and gestures of driver and passenger, trying to see where their hands were resting. They didn't appear to be scrambling or overly fidgeting, which was a good sign. I approached the driver's window with the utmost caution, trying not to focus on either the driver or passenger too long. I had to be alert. I can honestly say that any concern I had about staying awake was long gone.

I stayed back from the driver's window, which forced him to look over his left shoulder just to see me. My flashlight was partially blinding him from getting a good look at me, which gave me a small safe advantage if he happened to be armed. He already had his driver's license ready, and I told him I stopped him for the burned out headlight. The driver didn't appear terribly nervous, but the passenger seemed very concerned. He seemed even more concerned when I recognized him. I had been his school bus driver years earlier! Still, I did not see the connection to anything criminal yet.

I was examining the driver's license and noticed the driver had not given me the registration to the car he was driving. I sometimes let this one go because I can run the license tag, but this time I asked the driver to give it to me. He reached for the glove compartment, and as a precaution I slowly moved my right hand to the handle of my Berretta 92 pistol, which was in my safety holster at my side. When the driver opened the glove compartment, several twelve-gauge shotgun shells fell out onto the passenger floorboard!

At that point, the adrenaline began to pump, and I asked the driver to exit the vehicle and stand with me. I also asked him if he minded if I searched his car. Remarkably, his only response was "go ahead." I called for an assist car and advised my communications person why. They rushed a car my way as I patted both driver and passenger down for concealed weapons. Both were un-armed.

I directed the driver and passenger to stand in front of their car as I shined my light into it. The first things that caught my eye were two ski-masks with eyeholes cut out and two pairs of black gloves. I then noticed something that sent me over the edge of my red-alert mode.

Shining my light on the driver's floorboard, I noticed the wooden handle of something under the seat. I reached in and pulled the handle out. It was attached to a sawed-off, loaded twelve-gauge shotgun. I immediately placed the driver under arrest as my assist car arrived, and I motioned for my assist car to detain the passenger. By this time my adrenaline was in full pump, I had lost a partial bit of my hearing, and I had a low hum in both of my ears.

What I wasn't aware of at the moment was that the tactical police squad had been staked out at the nearby convenience mart on Wendover Avenue, less than a quarter of a mile from where I stopped the teenagers. The tact squad had received a tip that the convenience mart was going to be robbed. I had unknowingly stopped the very suspects who were moments away from committing armed robbery at a convenience mart! I would like to say that the tactical police squad was appreciative of my diligence, but that would not be true. I cut in on their effort that night and took quite a bit of excitement away from their quiet evening.

KEEPING ALERT AS A CHRISTIAN

You may ask what that story has to do with our lives as Christians, or maybe you have it figured out. We each have a duty before God to stay alert, sober, and diligent to the schemes and plotting of Satan in our lives. Satan wants you to fall and ultimately wants you to fail, but we must be ever mindful of his cunning and conniving tactics. Just as I recognized the passenger in the car on that fateful night, we fight and war with an enemy we know and are familiar with.

Peter warns us that Satan is just waiting for us to drop our guard and expose our weaknesses.

Be self-controlled and alert. Your enemy the devil prowls around like a roaring lion looking for someone to devour (1 Peter 5:8).

The night I encountered and foiled the suspected robbers-to-be, I was tired and fatigued from a very long night, but I didn't have the luxury of dropping my guard. To tell the truth, I firmly believe that the only reason I am alive to type these words is because my guard was up. As a believer in Jesus Christ, you will find that Satan has your whole lifetime to wait for you to relax or drop your guard. He looks for those moments in your life where you don't study the Bible or pray. He waits for a crisis to invade your marriage so that he can influence a compromised mind and heart. He watches to find your weaknesses; he will not relent or ease up. Satan and his helpers are the most interested in finding where you will succumb to his attacks, and he doesn't have to look that hard with many of us. Many Christians have relaxed their guard and are willing participants in his schemes.

Satan needs no enhanced interrogation techniques to break you; all he needs is to observe and wait for his moment, knowing it will come.

KNOW YOUR WEAKNESS AND CONFRONT IT!

The night of the shotgun encounter, my biggest enemy was fatigue. I could have easily ignored the car and done nothing, but it may have placed some of my brothers in blue in harm's way even more than I. As Christians, we must stay active and alert to our weaknesses and never give in to complacency.

The Bible teaches us how to be ready in Ephesians 6:10-18, where Paul shows us step by step how to be prepared for Satan's attacks. Always be ready and alert because even the most "spiritual" person you know can become weak if they become complacent or tired. Always be prepared to take defensive measures in your everyday activities. If you are prone to inappropriate relationships, then take measures to cease what makes you fall. If you are an addict, then seek out the right biblical help and get accountability in your life. This list could go on, but we must not give in or give up!

DISCUSSION QUESTIONS

1. Based on this chapter, are there any inappropriate or dangerous relationships in your life that you need to address or discuss?

2. Is there a person of the opposite gender that you would rather share your day with in place of your spouse?

3. Based on this chapter, what precautions do you need to take?

4. What is your biggest weakness right now?

INSIGHTS

MARRIAGE TRIAGE

God's Grace Never Leaves

Own Your Sins and Failures

Document Your Thoughts and Experiences

Counsel with Godly People

Adapt To Your Circumstances

Respond Biblically

Endure Through Your Circumstances

Shield Your Heart

I glorify Thee on the earth, having accomplished the work which Thou hast given Me to do.

~John 17:4

CHAPTER ELEVEN
THE REAL PURPOSE

When considering a biblical response to your circumstances, you could believe that the Bible is nothing more than a works-based rule book for life. You could read page after page, thinking you will never be able to live up to all of these instructions.

It is easy to miss the real purpose. When you are trying to be **grace**-filled and forgiving to your spouse, it seems so one-sided and unfair. You **own** up to your sins and failures, and yet your spouse acknowledges nothing but your wrongs. You have **documented** how you feel and **counseled** with godly people, and yet your spouse calls you weak and mindless. You see yourself as having **adapted** quite well to your circumstances, and your **responses** have truly been biblical, but where is the reward? You are **enduring** and persevering through your marriage crisis, but it feels likes no one is paying attention. Maybe you have even struggled in **shielding** your heart, but you endured and made it!

BEING EQUIPPED

You have no doubt noticed that this book was less about finding a stream-lined way to reconnect with your spouse and more about how to nurture a closer walk with Christ. It was written to adequately equip you to endure the trials and suffering in your marriage. This book has provided a way for you to address the sin and strongholds that have held you back from being all God wants you to be. It has never been your spouse that has held you back, but you. You stand alone before God without excuse.

So many couples have entered my office ill-equipped to take care of one of the most precious possessions in their earthly lives—their own hearts. Through this book, I pray that you have slowly turned your eyes away from your spouse and taken an uninterrupted and reflective view of your own heart and life. To be without excuse before God means deep inward assessments that never leaves the recesses of your own heart.

THE PURPOSE

Even though you must sometimes follow biblical direction when it doesn't seem logical, there is a purpose in everything Christians are called to do. The purpose isn't veiled but clearly seen in the Gospels. Jesus told His disciples that their faith would be tested and stretched through their trials and tribulations. Even when there appeared to be looming defeat in times of trial, Jesus was always in control.

"Behold an hour is coming and has already come, for you to be scattered, each to his own home, and to leave Me alone; and yet I am not alone, because the Father is with Me. These things I have spoken to you, that in Me you may have peace. In the world you have tribulation, but take courage; I have overcome the world" (John 16:32-33).

The sustenance in our trials comes through our obedience. It is the fruit of a life lived in obedience to the instructions mapped out for us throughout God's all-sufficient Scriptures. We were made *to glorify God in all that we do*, regardless of the cost (Colossians 3:23). Jesus encapsulated this in His priestly prayer with His disciples.

I glorify Thee on the earth, having accomplished the work which Thou hast given Me to do. And now, glorify Thou Me together with Thyself, Father, with the glory which I had with Thee before the world was" (John 17:4-5, KJV).

Jesus was plotted against, betrayed, defamed, and denied, but in the end, He and the Father were glorified! Do you understand that when your spouse betrays and shatters your heart that you can still glorify God by the way you choose to react? Jesus has given you a guarantee that He will never leave you! Those moments when you feel all alone, He is still there. The moments you feel cheated, He is still there. Those moments when you feel like you can't go on, He is still there. No matter what or how you feel, **He is**!

I know, O Lord, that thy judgments are righteous, and that in faithfulness Thou hast afflicted me. O may Thy loving kindness comfort me, according to Thy word to Thy servant (Psalm 119:75-76, KJV).

JOHN AND RACHEL

Years had passed since John and Rachel experienced and endured the painful trial in their marriage. However, Rachel's thoughts had returned to the woman with whom John had been emotionally involved. Rachel didn't feel that she was tempted to dwell, but no matter how many Scriptures she recited in her head, she couldn't shake the woman's face from her thoughts. Rachel even told John what she had been experiencing, and he felt helpless and guilty for Rachel's dilemma. The other woman, named Leah, lived in a nearby city, and

Rachel was losing sleep as she tried to figure out how to shake the thoughts of Leah from her mind. It's not as though Rachel had been dwelling regularly on Leah. In fact, she could count the number of times she had thought about her over the past several years. Rachel felt that she had forgiven Leah and moved on. It just didn't make any logical sense to think about what lay in the past. It wasn't even an event that was being triggered by a place or situation—just thoughts running through her mind about Leah.

As Rachel was driving home from work on a late summer's day, she was praying and asking God for clarification. A sudden realization overwhelmed her. "No God! No! Please don't let this be what you are doing! Of all the emotions you could place upon me, Lord, you chose to burden my heart for Leah?" Rachel wasn't even sure that Leah still lived in the same nearby city.

On a sunny Friday, Rachel called Leah's old workplace and found out that she was still employed there. Without telling John where she was going, Rachel made her plans and left. She arrived in Leah's city about mid-day while still planning exactly what she was going to do or say. She stopped by a local greeting card store and began looking for a card to fit the occasion. Rachel jokingly let some outlandish rhymes run through her head of what she wished the card would say, but deep down she truly felt sorry for Leah. When Rachel finally chose an appropriate card and took it to the counter to pay, the clerk commented, "I got that same card for someone the other day." Rachel smiled and replied, "That's nice, but I am pretty sure you purchased your card under a different set of circumstances."

Rachel left the store and went next door to the local bookstore. She knew what book she wanted to purchase but was very concerned that it wouldn't be in stock. She was hoping to find one of her favorite books on marriage. Rachel searched high and low, but she could not find a copy of the book. Hoping that at least one copy could be found, she asked for assistance from a clerk. The clerk looked on the computer for a copy of the book, and it appeared one copy was in stock. Rachel anxiously awaited a status near the coffee stand. Fifteen minutes later, the clerk returned with a copy of the book. Then Rachel chose a gift bag for the book.

Rachel somberly walked through the parking lot and sat in her car. She bowed her head and began to pray for Leah's life, family, and husband. She prayed that God would make Leah receptive to an offer of unsolicited forgiveness. Rachel felt that Leah needed to know that there was no animosity or ill will. Rachel didn't want Leah to live the rest of her life without knowing that Rachel didn't hate her. Rachel could be a testimony of Christian love and forgiveness unlike anyone Leah knew. Rachel even hoped for a chance to talk to Leah about a relationship with Jesus Christ. Would Leah be receptive?

While still in the parking lot of the bookstore, Rachel began writing in the card she had purchased.

Leah,

I just wanted to take a moment and let you know that you have been on my mind, and I have been praying for you. I long for you to know all that Christ can do in your life if you let Him. I also want you to know that just as John forgave me for failing as a wife, I totally forgive you and desire for you to have a fulfilling marriage. I pray that this book would provide some tools for you to begin your journey to becoming the wife God wants you to be.

Sincerely,
Rachel

It was late in the day, and Rachel knew she didn't have long before Leah would be leaving her job. She arrived at Leah's worksite at 4pm and walked down the office hallway. She arrived at Leah's office door and noticed the light was off and no one was inside. Clearly, Leah had already left for the day. Rachel placed the bag containing the card and book on Leah's desk and said a short prayer.

Rachel walked to her car and noticed a strange sensation in her chest and legs. It was a feeling she had not experienced in the past two weeks. Rachel literally felt like a weight had been lifted off of her. The burden was released!

THE GENUINE FRUIT OF OBEDIENCE

When it comes to marriage, our society has "happily ever after" defined as the white picket fence, big house, and lots of money. The indicator of happiness is also judged by the lack of issues and hard times in a couple's marriage. The irony of Rachel's experience happens to be that she came to a place of fulfillment through demonstrating **grace** that occurred when she showed mercy and forgiveness to John. She **owned** her sins and failures by confessing to John and God her own faults and seeking his forgiveness. Rachel spent time **documenting** her feelings and insights, and **counseling** with godly people. She even did a good job **adapting** to her circumstances, and praying that her **responses** would be Christ-like even when she was in the depths of pain. Rachel **endured** her hurt and pain, and she put protective boundaries in place to **shield** her heart.

None of Rachel's biblical actions led to monetary prosperity or worldly blessings. Jesus tells Christians to be careful of this sort of motivation.

And He said to them, "Beware and be on your guard against every form of greed; for not even when one has an abundance does his life consist of his possessions" (Luke 12:15).

You may wonder what the real fruit of obedience is supposed to be if it isn't monetary. Rachel hinted at it when she mentioned that her actions brought ease and comfort to her life. Rachel honored and glorified Christ by conducting herself biblically throughout her marriage crisis. She had many failures through the crisis, but she never gave up. Both John and Rachel were refined into more mature and disciplined followers of Jesus Christ. Both of them learned how to have genuine contentment and peace in the midst of their trials (Philippians 4:11-13).

Not that I speak from want, for I have learned to be content in whatever circumstances I am. I know how to get along with humble means, and I also know how to live in prosperity; in any and every circumstance I have learned the secret of being filled and going hungry, both of having abundance and suffering need. I can do all things through Him (Christ) who strengthens me (Philippians 4:11-13).

WHAT IF MY SPOUSE NEVER CHANGES?

Some books may teach you how to meet your spouse's needs in the form of love languages and love tanks, but what if there is still no response? I am not minimizing the importance of knowing that type of information, but you need not become disillusioned if your spouse fails to acknowledge your efforts. There are many moments in our Christian life that aren't met with praise and reciprocation, and we need to be content with this outcome. There are many prosperity philosophies and movements out there that have left an immense wake of disillusionment in its followers. Understandably, disillusioned Christians find great rest in the godly principles we have discussed throughout this book. Much of the praise and thanks we receive may not materialize in our earthly existence. I hope you understand that I have not been appealing to the "feel good" crowd throughout this book, but to spouses who are hurting and are receptive to true hope.

WE HAVE A JUMPER!

It was a busy second shift in the early nineties. It was late in the afternoon, and I was on my way to a non-emergency type of call. The traffic was heavier than usual on this particular day, and my entire squad had been hopping from call to call ever since we went on duty. It wasn't uncommon to be busy on second shift, and we spent much of the afternoons doing traffic accident investigations and cleaning up from the shift that just went off-duty. I was traveling west on East Bessemer Avenue when something caught my eye. There was a hysterical, screaming woman running in traffic on the bridge of East Bessemer Avenue, which was over U.S. Highway 29! I picked up my radio microphone and told police communications that I would be checking on the woman. I remember calling it in as a potential 10-96 (mental) person.

Hoping to prevent cars from accidentally striking the woman, I positioned my police cruiser in the right lane of the roadway and activated my blue emergency lights. Although I was ready for just about any scenario, I did not anticipate the woman's reaction to my presence. She ran straight for the bridge railing and began climbing over the cement barrier, which could only lead to a sixty foot plummet onto highway U.S. 29. I had no time to call for help or get further assistance. This was a life and death situation, and it required my immediate response!

I sprinted twenty yards, dodging around several stopped cars. I was so focused on the woman that I probably came close to getting hit, myself. All I could imagine was seeing the woman's lifeless body sprawled on the highway below if I didn't get to her in time. As I reached the cement barrier, I was able to grab her arm, and I supported her entire weight as her legs dangled above the busy highway. What made this situation even worse? The woman had no desire to be saved. She wanted to plummet to the pavement, and I was the only obstacle to her primary goal! With strength I did not know I possessed, I was able to pull her back onto the bridge as she scratched and flailed her arms in an attempt to break free. I literally pulled her shirt half-way off as I wrestled her to the pavement and placed her in handcuffs. I could feel my earlier meal of drive-thru food sitting in my chest, and I was exhausted. By that time, several cars had stopped to assist me, but the fight was already over. In a matter of seconds, I had managed to save the life of an ungrateful woman whose family to this day has never said or written so much as a thank you.

I took the lady to county mental health services, where they did an emergency assessment on her condition. I remember reporting the whole incident to my sergeant. My captain later deemed the incident as unworthy of a life-saving medal. That's right, not one additional word was ever breathed about the incident. I had saved a woman's life, and all I had to show for it was a small mention on the commander's summary and numerous fingernail scratches across my face and arms.

What if my decision to help this woman had been determined solely by whether she would be thankful for my efforts? If that had been the case, the woman would currently be in a cemetery in the vicinity of Greensboro, North Carolina. Because God placed me in the right place at the right time, the woman is still living, and I pray she is doing well. I can live without a thank you, but she cannot live without breath.

I am sympathetic toward any desire to slap your spouse's face for the way they may have treated you. I am even sorry that you may be one of the spouses who may never see your mate change into what God desires. I am sorry if you have a desire for reciprocation that is in a current state of constipation. I am burdened by the fact that you may have a spouse who won't read a pamphlet, much less this entire book, but I am proud of you! You are seeking to be what God requires, regardless of the actions of your spouse. You have been placed in the life of your spouse to be an example for such a time as this.

CONCLUSION

For the past twelve chapters, I have been letting down my walls and letting you get to know me for the purpose of earning your trust. I have tried to get you as comfortable and relaxed as possible by letting you know that I have walked through most of the valleys in one form or another that we have discussed.

I pray that I have earned your confidence throughout this book, but most of all, I hope you have begun to learn that God deserves your total confidence and loyalty. I don't believe I could have been any more frank or open about your marriage issues. I may have made some of you furious at times, but because you know I love and care for you as my Christian friends, it appears you have read to the end of the book.

Whether you are finishing this book with your spouse or alone, I leave you with the comfort of knowing that Christ loves and cares for you as His child. Even when you have felt alone in your grief, Christ has never left your side.

Let your character be free from the love of money, being content with what you have; for He Himself has said, "I will never desert you, nor will I ever forsake you" (Hebrews 13:5).

THE WOUNDS ARE STABILIZED

If we ever meet on the street or at a conference, there is one thing I want you to tell me. Have your emotional wounds been stabilized? Do you really understand that **God cares**? I pray that as you walk through your marriage crisis, these simple steps have opened up a way for you to navigate through your situation in a God-honoring and Christ-like manner. I leave you with Paul's words.

To the only wise God, through Jesus Christ, be the glory forever. Amen (Romans 16:27).

APPENDIX

MARRIAGE TRIAGE QUICK-START GUIDE

Let me express my deepest sympathy for the spouse who just picked up this book and flipped to the Quick-Start Guide. You feel as if there is a gaping hole in your chest where your heart has been cruelly torn out. Because your marriage is in critical condition, you don't have time to linger in tears. You came here seeking immediate help and guidance.

SLOW DOWN!

Whatever your crisis may be, don't assume that it requires an immediate behavioral reaction—except under certain extreme circumstances. As a former police officer, I must say that if you are in an abusive or imminent life-threatening situation, then you need to act quickly to protect yourself.

However, most of the spouses reading this book aren't there. You are frustrated, hurting, and shocked with no idea how to react. Your life has just been changed forever, either by your own actions or the choices of your spouse. For this reason I direct you to slow down and stop assuming that you must take immediate emergency action every moment of the day. That festering sense will drive you to do things without thinking or weighing the consequences. For men, it may be the desire to seek retaliation or restitution. For women, it may be to confront the offender or to run away and hide. The choices are limitless, but the urgency to act is unfounded. Move, think, and choose both slowly and deliberately. Don't make choices that will create an even bigger problem in your already critical situation. I encourage you to write down the following verses and place them within arm's reach for the next few months, if not longer.

Better is a poor man who walks in his integrity than he who is perverse in speech and is a fool. Also it is not good for a person to be without knowledge, and he who makes haste (rushes) with his feet errs (Proverbs 19:1-2).

You need to get alone and be very still while you prepare your heart and mind for a difficult and uncertain journey. No one knows how this crisis will play out but Jesus, and you will need to get to a place where you are okay with such a journey. If you are not there yet, that's fine. We will take this journey one slow and deliberate step at a time. We will use Scripture, personal lessons, prayer, and maybe a little humor. Yes, your ability to laugh and chuckle will be restored; they are not gone for good.

Use the *insights* page at the end of each chapter to record your thoughts. To get started, the acronym we will work from is **GOD CARES**.

God's Grace Never Leaves

Own Your Sins and Failures

Document Your Thoughts and Experiences

Counsel with Godly People

Adapt To Your Circumstances

Respond Biblically

Endure Through Your Circumstances

Shield Your Heart

GOD'S GRACE NEVER LEAVES

Rely on God. His grace will help you through each moment even when you're tempted to act out emotionally. God will guide you to act in obedience to Him through His grace and mercy. Never forget the grace that God has shown to you by forgiving and forgetting your past transgressions. Even when you can't forget your own sins, God has already removed them. Remember this grace as you make day-to-day decisions on how to carry on when life seems so full of hurt and emptiness. Even if your spouse continues in their sins, you can choose to act in a way to show grace and honor to God's gift to you.

And God is able to make all grace abound toward you, that you, always having all sufficiency in all things, have abundance for every good work (2 Corinthians 9:8).

When your emotions run wild and leave you in a very vulnerable position, only by the application of God's matchless grace will you be able to make rational and biblical choices.

OWN YOUR SINS AND FAILURES

The temptation will be to focus on your spouse and rationalize away your own mistakes and sins in the marriage. Be the Christian spouse who takes responsibility for both your current and future actions. Pray that God will give you humility through this marriage crisis.

The fear of the Lord is the instruction for wisdom, and before honor comes humility (Proverbs 15:33).

The Bible says that God opposes the proud but gives grace to the humble. You must resist the temptation to assert yourself and make demands, thinking you are entitled to some form of emotional retribution. Acting biblically means acknowledging your sins and praying for the condition of your spouse's heart, regardless of their actions. Whether or not you feel that the love is gone is irrelevant. You are not in a frame of mind to determine this, even when you have evidence of the most obvious offenses.

But He gives a greater grace. Therefore it says, "God opposes the proud, but gives grace to the humble" (James 4:6).

DOCUMENT YOUR FEELINGS AND EXPERIENCES

Keep a detailed journal about your experiences and feelings while going through this trial. Search out and document Scripture that brings comfort and guidance to you in your pain. Follow David's example. Throughout the Psalms, when David was in great emotional pain, he wrote many Psalms that revealed his state of mind. In the end, he would see that God had not abandoned him. You are seeing and experiencing things you need to remember and reflect upon, and journaling will help you do this. Writing about your experiences will allow the Holy Spirit to guide you in recording the thoughts and revelations that are most important. You are only the compiler, while Christ is the coordinator, counselor, consoler, and consolidator.

But the Helper, the Holy Spirit, whom the Father will send in My name, He will teach you all things, and bring to remembrance all that I said to you (John 14:26).

Jesus taught the disciples this principle when He explained to them how they would reflect and recall so many details of their time with Him. The great news for you, if you are a believer and follower of Jesus Christ, is that you have the Holy Spirit indwelling your life. If you wonder why there are moments that you just inexplicably know things are going to be all right, it's the Holy Spirit. He is the one who comforts and guides your thoughts and matters. The Holy Spirit will help you to bring order to your chaotic life! The Holy Spirit is an organizer of chaos.

Another reason to journal through the pain and agony you are feeling is to curtail an inappropriate habit of telling your story to everyone you know. Not everyone needs to know what you are going through at this point; also, well-intentioned people can offer some pretty weak advice such as "God wants you to be happy" or "kick your spouse to the curb!" In your writing, you can focus on telling God how you feel. Cast all your cares on Jesus during this time and condition yourself to pray more and share less. When friends ask you how you are doing, you needn't feel obligated to make them sit through a detailed saga.

Casting all your anxiety upon Him, because He cares for you (1 Peter 5:8).

COUNSEL WITH GODLY PEOPLE

Consider the following Psalm as a warning to avoid seeking counsel from ungodly friends:

How blessed is the man who does not walk in the counsel of the wicked, nor stand in the path of sinners, nor sit in the seat of scoffers (Psalm 1:1).

You may have some great and sincere friends who want to protect you from further pain, but you need to be sure that they are going to guide you biblically. Seek out a godly counselor who will guide you and hold you accountable for your actions and reactions. Filter all advice through the Holy Scriptures.

Trust in the Lord with all your heart, and do not lean on your own understanding. In all your ways acknowledge Him, and He will make your paths straight (Proverbs 3:5-6).

We are told in the Bible to trust and acknowledge God in all areas of our life, and that includes the area of a broken marriage. Seek out a godly counselor, pastor, or seasoned Christian mentor who is not afraid to be brutally honest with you. Such a guide will comfort you in Scripture and chasten you with love and compassion. Check the appendix of this book for help with locating a Bible-based resource during this difficult season of your life.

ADAPT TO YOUR CIRCUMSTANCES

Whether your circumstances have come about as a result of poor choices, sin, or neither, none of that is relevant to your response as a Christian. Now is not the time to wonder and fret over why God is allowing you to experience such great pain and suffering. There are responsibilities to address, bills to be paid, and maybe even children to take care of, so it is important not to lose all perspective in your situation. David was in a similar frame of mind after his rebellious son, Absalom, was killed.

David was melancholy and had begun to spend all of his time dwelling on the death of his son, and it affected the entire kingdom. Morale was at an all-time low. There were many kingdom matters to attend to, and something needed to change in David's approach to his circumstances. It finally fell upon Joab to confront David about his downcast attitude.

"Now therefore arise, go out and speak kindly to your servants, for I swear by the Lord, if you do not go out, surely not a man will pass the night with you, and this will be worse for you than all the evil that has come upon you from your youth until now" (2 Samuel 19:7).

Joab confronted David with some urgent and immediate truths. Joab told him it was time to adapt godly habits and actions to the situation he was in. There were people watching him to see how he reacted to his circumstances, and although he was hurting, he needed to be strong in the Lord! Joab told David that men would not be there to sit by him night after night with no commitment from him to change his ways and respond in a way that honors God.

You need to embrace the concept that no matter what happens in your marriage, you will adapt and accept the principle that God is in control even while you feel your life spiraling out of control. Be adaptable to your circumstances right now and believe that God will never leave or forsake you.

To adapt biblically to your circumstances is to let your commitment to Christ subdue your fleshly emotions. When we hurt, we can easily fall back to old ways, which is ironic because it is a time when we have the best opportunity to get closer to Christ. Just focus on adapting in a way that would honor Christ in your weakened state.

Therefore gird your minds for action, keep sober in spirit, fix your hope completely on the grace to be brought to you at the revelation of Jesus Christ. As obedient children, do not be conformed to the former lusts which were yours in your ignorance, but like the Holy One who called you, be holy yourselves also in all your behavior; because it is written, "YOU SHALL BE HOLY, FOR I AM HOLY" (1 Peter 1:13-16).

RESPOND BIBLICALLY

How do you respond in a way that honors God when your world is crumbling around you? The world would tell you that all this religious stuff is nonsense. Your spouse may have shattered any trust in your marriage, and here I am telling you to respond biblically? Quite frankly, if I were the only one telling you this, you wouldn't have to listen, but the Bible says it also!

Respond to your crisis based on what the Bible guides you to do. Resist the temptation to respond emotionally and negatively even though it makes more sense. At this early stage in the crisis, I recommend that you find someone to hold you accountable for acting in a way that honors God before you make any preventable mistakes.

How blessed are those whose way is blameless, who walk in the law of the Lord (Psalm 119:1).

In order to respond biblically, you may need to change your current direction. It may take some time to seek the right counsel to address all your sins, but this is when you need to take the first step. Even if you aren't the betrayer or adulterer, you haven't been given a pass from examining your life and seeing what areas of your Christian walk need strengthening. Trust me when I say that the trial that you are in will bring out every sinful flaw you struggle with. Paul said in Acts that we don't just need to talk about repenting but to change whatever is necessary in order to demonstrate the repentance.

To the Gentiles, that they should repent and turn to God, performing deeds appropriate to repentance (Acts 26:20).

It may seem enticing to respond sinfully and bathe yourself in your emotionally sinful nature, but I urge you to act in a way that would honor your Lord Jesus Christ. Turn from the things that would make you sinful and dirty. Respond in a way that God would deem appropriate.

ENDURE THROUGH YOUR TRIAL

Trials don't make sense, and yet that doesn't prevent their frequent presence in our lives. When we feel betrayed, lonely, and compromised, it is tempting to throw in the towel and give up. Yet, you need to keep running this crazy race while you allow God to reveal the areas of your circumstances He knows you can handle. God may even be waiting on you to practice your faith, but the one thing we can be sure of is that He is in no way giving you permission to quit. You are hurt, shaken, beaten, and pressed down, but God will make a way for you to see the future again! You must endure!

If you are a child of God, then He will protect you through this alleged dead end in your life. The strength to endure through this trial will come from God's never-missing presence.

The Lord is good; A stronghold in the day of trouble, and He knows those who take refuge in Him (Nahum 1:7-8).

Nahum said this during some pretty perilous times. Nineveh was the target of the prophecy. Nineveh, the capitol of Assyria, had been ruthless to Israel. The Ninevites were masters of torture and mayhem. Assyria was the same nation that carried Samaria out into bondage by putting huge fish-hooks in their mouths. As ruthless as Assyria was to Israel, God told His people not to worry about the outcome because He would take care of them. He would be their refuge.

Right this very minute you are hurting and alone, but I know where to send you for endurance and refuge. God is your refuge and strength, and you can endure this trial!

God is our refuge and strength, A very present help in trouble (Psalm 46:1-2).

SHIELD YOUR HEART

Your emotions can deceive you when your heart is virtually in pieces on the floor. Several wives have come to sit in my office, wives who had literally reached a point of "done-ness" that drove them to intentionally seek out a man who would appreciate them as opposed to ignoring them. It's a very easy mindset to place yourself in when you feel like your spouse no longer cares. I refer to this state of mind as more of a survival mode, but the end result is self-destruction and possibly the destruction of the family as well.

It is very easy to let your emotions overshadow your commitment to Christ when you are hurting so badly from unfaithfulness and betrayal—so much so that you can begin to rationalize away the walls that protect your heart from sinful outside influences. When you think another person of the opposite sex may understand how you feel even more than your spouse, it is tempting to form sinful emotional connections. You wouldn't go to bed each night in a crime-infested neighborhood with the doors to your home unlocked, so why are you any less careful with the shields that guard your heart?

As a result, we are no longer to be children tossed here and there by waves and carried about by every wind of doctrine, by trickery of men, by craftiness in deceitful scheming (Ephesians 4:14).

When Paul wrote this, he was speaking with the church at Ephesus. He spelled out for them what to be on guard against and what to both intentionally do and not do. Right now you may just crave attention from someone who understands and cares to listen, but your emotions can compromise your judgment.

For those still dazed and confused, let me make it very simple. Stay away from kind and listening ears of the opposite sex—even those you consider as friends and acquaintances—regardless of the circumstances. Obviously this excludes blood-related family members, but I am referring to people of the opposite sex whose opinions you value more than your spouse's. Filter all the advice you receive through the lens of Scripture.

NOTES

MARRIAGE TRIAGE

1. The **Biblical Counseling Moment** airs locally in Charlotte, NC, and mp3s can be downloaded at TrumpetforGod.org. The episodes can also be subscribed to through iTunes.
2. Stephen was asked to discuss a case from 1990 involving a murder in Greensboro, North Carolina. He has written an article on the experience which can be viewed at stephengoode.com.
3. *Oxford American Dictionary* (New York: Oxford University Press, 1980)
4. Walter A. Elwell and Philip Wesley Comfort, Tyndale Bible Dictionary, Tyndale reference library (Wheaton, Ill.: Tyndale House Publishers, 2001), 550.
5. Cheryl & Jeff Scruggs, *I Do Again* (Colorado Springs: Waterbrook Press, 2008), 38.
6. Jeremy Lelek, *Association of Biblical Counselors* (ChristianCounseling.com) ABC is a great source for information on biblical counselors.
7. E. Joseph Deering, *Houston Chronicle,* 2005, Additional information at http://www.groupbuilder.net/uploads/friends_for_Clara_harris/news.php?release_num=1130

8. Timothy Boczkowski is currently imprisoned in Pamlico Correctional Institute in North Carolina as a first degree murder inmate. All information discussed in this book is from the public record.
http://webapps6.doc.state.nc.us/opi/viewoffender.do?method=view&offenderID=0553913&obscure=Y&listpage=1&listurl=pagelistoffendersearchresults&searchLastName=boczkowski

RESOURCES
BOOK RECOMMENDATIONS

MARRIAGE
Sacred Marriage and other titles by Gary Thomas
The Power of a Praying series by Stormie Omartian
I Do Again by Cheryl and Jeff Scruggs
Intimate Issues by Linda Dillow and Lorraine Pintus
Love & Respect by Emerson Eggerichs
War of Words by Paul David Tripp
Love Must be Tough by Dr. James Dobson
Torn Asunder: Recovering from an Extramarital Affair by Dave Carder
Shattered Vows by Debra Laaser

TRUSTED INTERNET RESOURCES
Stephen Goode's Ministry Resources
stephengoode.com
trumpetforGod.org
Dr. Alex McFarland Religion and Culture Expert
alexmcfarland.com

RPM Ministries
rpmministries.org
The Center for Evangelical Spirituality
garythomas.com
Northside Baptist Charlotte Ministries
northsidecharlotte.com
Hope Matters Marriage Ministries, Inc.
hopeformarriages.com

ABOUT THE AUTHOR
STEPHEN GOODE

STEPHEN GOODE IS THE PASTOR of Biblical Counseling and Senior Adult Ministries at Northside Baptist Church in Charlotte, North Carolina. He is a graduate of Trinity Bible College and Theological Seminary with a B.A. in biblical counseling, and he is completing his master's work in the same field. Steve is the host of The Biblical Counseling Moment[1] aired on the radio and iTunes podcast. Episodes were downloaded more than 100,000 times in 2011. Steve also hosts the weekly Blogtalk Radio show online. Steve served eleven years in North Carolina as a sworn police officer for the Greensboro Police Department, where he gained extensive experience working closely with families in crisis. Steve was interviewed on Discovery ID in a true crime series called The Devil You Know[2] (Make Believe Media Inc.). He has been married to April Durham Goode since 1994, and they have two children. Born in Tuscaloosa, Alabama, Stephen has lived in North Carolina since 1978. Stephen's burden and passion is to lead married couples and individuals into a deeper walk with Jesus Christ.

For more information about
Stephen Goode
&
Marriage Triage
please visit:

stephengoode.com
info@marriagetriage.com
www.facebook.com/steve.goode
www.facebook.com/MarriageTriage
@stephen_goode

For more information about
AMBASSADOR INTERNATIONAL
please visit:

www.ambassador-international.com
@AmbassadorIntl
www.facebook.com/AmbassadorIntl